Using Bibliotherapy
in Clinical Practice

Recent Titles in
Contributions in Psychology

Using Bibliotherapy in Clinical Practice

A Guide to Self-Help Books

John T. Pardeck

Contributions in Psychology, Number 22

Greenwood Press
Westport, Connecticut • London

Library of Congress Cataloging-in-Publication Data

Pardeck, John T.
Using bibliotherapy in clinical practice : a guide to self-help
books / John T. Pardeck.
p.   cm. — (Contributions in psychology, ISSN 0736-2714 ; no.
22)
Includes bibliographical references and indexes.
ISBN 0-313-27991-8 (alk. paper)
1. Bibliotherapy. 2. Self-help techniques — Bibliography. 3. Life
skills — Bibliography. I. Title. II. Series.
[DNLM: 1. Bibliotherapy — methods. 2. Self Care — methods —
abstracts. 3. Adaptation, Psychological — abstracts. 4. Mental
Health — abstracts.   W1 CO778NHH no.22 1994 / WM 450.5.B5 P2263u
1994]
Z7204.S44P37 1994
[RC489.B48]
016.61689'166 — dc20
DNLM/DLC
for Library of Congress   93-20499

British Library Cataloguing in Publication Data is available.

Library of Congress Catalog Card Number: 93-20499
ISBN: 0-313-27991-8
ISSN: 0736-2714

First published in 1993

Greenwood Press, 88 Post Road West, Westport, CT 06881
An imprint of Greenwood Publishing Group, Inc.

Printed in the United States of America

The paper used in this book complies with the
Permanent Paper Standard issued by the National
Information Standards Organization (Z39.48-1984).

10 9 8 7 6 5 4 3 2 1

To Jean, Jamie, Jonathan

Contents

Preface

PURPOSE

The purpose of this book is to provide professionals in the field of mental health with readily available information on self-help books that can effectively be used with various clinical problems. The materials presented in the work can also be used by those not necessarily trained in clinical intervention; this group includes but is not limited to parents, teachers, and librarians. Those who simply wish to gain greater insight into a problem will find many of the books presented in this work useful.

The approach offered in the work is bibliotherapy. Bibliotherapy is an emerging clinical technique that is useful for treating various problems. Chapter 1 offers an overview of the bibliotherapeutic approach, who uses it in practice, and a detailed review of the literature on the topic of bibliotherapy.

Chapter 2 presents the clinical applications of bibliotherapy. This chapter covers the principles of bibliotherapy, how one can use the approach in practice, and examples of books dealing with various clinical topics.

The clinical topics covered in this work focus on chemical dependency, coping with change, family violence and dysfunctional families, parenting, personal growth, serious illness, social relationships, and divorce and blended families. There are over 400 annotated self-help books presented in this work that deal with these potential problem areas. Most of the books are written for the adult reader.

COVERAGE AND SCOPE

The books annotated in this work were mostly published in the mid 1980s to the present; a limited number of the books are from earlier time periods. The general criteria used for a book to be included were that:

1. The book had to be a self-help book that dealt with one or more of the topics covered in the work.

2. The book had to offer useful content on the problem area covered.

3. The book had to be clearly appropriate to the implementation of the bibliotherapeutic process.

Each of the chapters covering a problem area includes a synopsis to help acquaint the reader with that particular problem. These synopses are not meant to be inclusive of all that is known about a particular problem included in the work; rather they are intended to focus on what the author felt was the most important information available at this point in brief form.

ENTRIES

The annotated entries included are arranged in alphabetical order by the author's last name. Many of the annotated literary works focus on more than one clinical problem. However, the primary clinical problem covered in a given literary work determined the chapter under which it was included. For example, a book on family violence may include some content on chemical dependency. If the primary focus is on family violence, however, the book was placed in the chapter on this topic.

INDEXES

The Author Index is a guide to the individuals who wrote the books annotated in each chapter. The Title Index helps the reader locate a particular title. The numbers following the authors and titles in these two indexes refer to the books' main entry numbers within each of the eight chapters. A Subject Index allows the reader to refer to specific subjects covered in the annotated entries. Like the two other indexes, the Subject Index refers the reader to the appropriate entry numbers within each chapter.

Acknowledgments

The author would like to thank Terry Brown for her excellent editorial comments on the earlier drafts of the manuscript. The author also appreciates the encouragement of Jean Pardeck, Ruth Pardeck, Lois Musick, and Burl Musick.

1

Introduction

Starker (1986) notes that it is unrealistic for mental health workers to consider themselves as the primary source of mental health care in America society. Many people are turning to a less expensive and more readily accessible alternative–the self-help book. Numerous books are now available on anxiety, alcoholism, and sexual dysfunction, as well as numerous other clinical problems. There is nothing to suggest that the expansion of the self-help book industry will abate.

The emergence of the self-help book is not necessarily a recent phenomenon. Self-help books for many years have been a part of the American culture. Starker (1986) reports that Samuel Thompson and Sylvester Graham, for example, had a popular health crusade in the 1820s and 1830s using self-help works extolling the virtues of exercise, diet, and sanitation. In the latter nineteenth and early twentieth century, popular religious and health movements based on self-help books emerged (Starker, 1986). Into the twentieth century famous titles still known to many were published. These included Dale Carnegie's (1936) *How to Win Friends and Influence People* and Benjamin Spock's (1946) *The Pocket Book of Baby and Child Care.* The 1960s and 1970s witnessed an outpouring of self-help books on humanistic, interpersonal, and third force psychologies, particularly transactional analysis (Starker, 1986). Harris's (1968) *I'm OK-You're OK* and Berne's (1964) *Games People Play* were classic works in the area of transactional analysis. In the 1980s and 1990s self-help books have become even more popular (Pardeck, 1992). Given the expansion of the self-help book industry, surprisingly, there has been limited research covering professionals' observations of self-help consumers, professional prescription of self-help works, and the effectiveness of self-help books.

Rosen (1976) has expressed concern with the proliferation of self-help books: "Consumers run the risk of purchasing treatment programs that may be ineffective or harmful when used on a total nonprescriptive basis" (p. 140). Goldiamond (1976) responded to Rosen's position with the argument that it is unfair to single out self-help treatment books in this regard. Goldiamond suggests that the public, not necessarily professionals, must decide the merits of a work. Rosen (1976), in response, has called for some type of professional regulation of self-help books. There is little to suggest that the debate on self-help books will be resolved in the near future. What we can conclude, however, is that the use of self-help books is not going to abate, and that professionals and consumers need accurate information on their strengths and limitations. This work attempts to provide such information on self-help books by focusing on the following topics: (1) providing a definition of self-help books, (2) reviewing the history and research on self-help books, (3) overviewing the clinical applications of self-help books, and (4) a presentation of annotated books on core clinical problems confronting families and individuals in the 1990s.

DEFINITION OF THE SELF-HELP BOOK

Self-help books are part of the broad field of bibliotherapy. Bibliotherapy has been known by many names, including bibliocounseling, bibliopsychology, biblioeducation, biblioguidance, library therapeutics, biblioprophylaxis, tutorial group therapy, and literatherapy (Rubin, 1978). Berry (1978, p. 185) defines bibliotherapy "as a family of techniques for structuring an interaction between a facilitator and a participant . . . based on their mutual sharing of literature." Webster (1985, p. 148) defines bibliotherapy as guidance in the solution of personal problems through reading. A recent definition by Bernstein (1989, pp. 159–160) defines bibliotherapy as the self-examination and insights that are gained from reading, no matter what the source. The source can be fiction or nonfiction (in settings ranging from guidance in the library or classroom to formal psychotherapy), self-directed, or purely accidental (pp. 159–160). Barker (1987), in his book entitled *The Social Work Dictionary*, defines bibliotherapy as "the use of literature and poetry in the treatment of people with emotional or mental illness. Bibliotherapy is often used in social group work and group therapy and is reported to be effective with people of all ages, with people in institutions as well as outpatients, and with healthy people who wish to share literature as a means of personal growth and development" (p. 15). All of the above definitions share one common thread, that being bibliotherapy requires some form of reading, but not all agree if the reading should be fiction, nonfiction, or both. Self-help books are grouped under the nonfiction area; consequently, the following definition from Katz and Sternberg Katz (1985) will be used in this work:

> Guides, manuals, and general treatises that help an individual, or modify other wise understand his or her physical or personal characteristics. (p. XV)

This definition is a broad net and takes in everything from health to child care. Katz and Sternberg Katz (1985) conclude that even though such a definition includes many elements, for example, human relations to individual concerns, it hardly seems likely that the average reader is going to confuse a guide on child care with a how–to–fix–a–roof book. What is important about the Katz and

Sternberg Katz definition is that it is grounded in the bibliotherapy tradition; however, it is a specialized form of bibliotherapy that includes only nonfiction works.

HISTORY AND RESEARCH ON SELF-HELP BOOKS

Books have been used as preventive aids as far back as problems and books have existed. In ancient Greek times, the door of the library at Thebes bore the inscription, *Healing place of the Soul*. If we look to the nineteenth century within the United States, such books as the *McGuffey Readers* and *The New England Primer* were used not only as teaching tools, but also as instruments to build character and develop positive values in students.

In the United States during the 1930s, one of the earliest individuals to use reading as a tool for helping individuals deal with mental health issues was Dr. William C. Menninger. Dr. Menninger was also interested in how the layperson used popular literature in the areas of psychiatry and psychology, as well as the kinds of readings prescribed in psychiatric settings. He found, for example, that the book *The Human Mind*, a popular work by his brother Karl A. Menninger (1945), was widely used by many laypersons and mental health professionals as a tool for dealing with mental health problems. Given this positive reaction to *The Human Mind*, the Menningers became advocates of using bibliotherapy in treatment. In fact, many mental hospitals began offering bibliotherapy treatment as a program entirely in the hands of librarians (Starker, 1986). The Menningers advise against prescribing mental health literature to psychotic individuals, those with anxiety states or obsessional neuroses, and those in psychoanalysis. It was deemed most appropriate for milder neuroses, alcoholism, for relatives of patients, and for parents who needed help in child guidance (Starker, 1988).

Since the Menningers's endorsement of self-help books as a mental health tool, increasing numbers of mental health professionals have been found to use this emerging technology in treatment. During the 1960s and 1970s numerous self-help books were published. Presently millions of Americans use self-help books for dealing with numerous problems ranging from advice on diets to personal growth. Savage, Hollin, and Hayward (1990) also note that the use of self-help books in treatment has expanded in Great Britain. Rosen (1976), however, has noted that numerous self-help books lack adequate validation. Glasgow and Rosen (1978) analyzed 75 self-help books published in a five–year period that offered self-administered treatments for phobia, obesity, smoking, sexual dysfunction, child behavior problems, and inhibited assertiveness. What was alarming concerning their findings was that very few of these books had been tested for clinical effectiveness. Glasgow and Rosen (1979) in a subsequent paper identified more than 150 behavioral self-help manuals in print. They found that less than half had been evaluated in any way. Rosen (1981) later concluded that the quality of self-help books continues to decline and that many self-help book authors make incredible if not outrageous claims about their usefulness. Clearly, a critical issue related to the self-help book movement is how effective such books are. Rosen (1981) has even suggested that many of these works might well be dangerous because troubled people may rely on self-help books over needed clinical treatment. In fact, Rosen has called for the regulation of the self-help book industry.

What becomes critical at this juncture are: how widespread is the use of self-help books among mental health professionals, and what does research report on the effectiveness of self-help manuals? Giblin, Pardeck and Pardeck, and Starker offer findings on this important topic.

Giblin (1989) reported that self-help books were widely recommended by clinicians in the area of family therapy. He found that self-help books were primarily used with individuals (77 percent) and groups (23 percent) in treatment. The therapists generally made formal reading assignments over informal ones. They typically referred the client to a bookstore or library for finding the title used in treatment. Most of the therapists had specific goals in mind when making a reading assignment. In turn, the therapists closely monitored the clients' emotional responses to the readings and discussed them during therapy.

Pardeck and Pardeck (1987) found that social workers did not appear to use bibliotherapy as widely as counselors. Through a content analysis of articles published from 1980 to 1983 in *Social Casework* and *Social Work*, they discovered that only seven articles appeared on bibliotherapy in these leading social work journals. Specifically, *Social Casework* published five articles and *Social Work* only two. In turn, the *School Counselor* and *Elementary School Guidance and Counseling* published over 40 articles on the topic of bibliotherapy during the same time period. Pardeck and Pardeck concluded that school counselors appeared to be widely acquainted with bibliotherapy, as reflected through the published works in the two counseling journals. Social workers, conversely, had little access to information on bibliotherapy, at least in terms of what had been published on the topic in the two leading social work journals.

Recent research by Starker (1986) revealed that psychologists, psychiatrists, and internists routinely prescribed self-help books in their practice. The survey of these professional groups was conducted in the Seattle, Washington, metropolitan area; of the 146 questionnaires sent to psychologists, 105 were completed. The sample were asked to provide their impression regarding how frequently their clients used self-help books. The psychologists completing the survey responded that 11.4 percent used self-help books quite often, 37.1 percent often, 47.6 percent sometimes, 3.8 percent rarely, and 0 percent never. The psychologists were also asked how often they prescribed self-help books. Results revealed that 88.6 percent did recommend such works. In the recommending group, 53.7 percent did so occasionally, 23.7 percent often, and 22.6 percent regularly. The psychologists recommended them most often for parenting, relationships, and personal growth. All psychologists responding to the survey reported that self-help books were helpful, and none viewed them as harmful.

Starker found psychiatrists also used self-help books in their practice. In the survey, 97 of the 164 psychiatrists completed the questionnaires, indicating that 5.2 percent of patients read self-help books quite often, 26 percent often, 57.3 percent rarely, and 0 percent never. As for prescriptive practices, 58.8 percent reported prescribing self-help books as a supplement to intervention. However, 67.9 percent of these prescribers did so occasionally, 19.6 percent often, and 12.5

percent regularly. Only 2 percent of the responding psychiatrists viewed self-help books as harmful; 4.2 percent saw them as unhelpful, whereas the remaining respondents indicated that they were helpful in varying degrees.

Finally, Starker reported that of the 177 internists surveyed, 63 completed the survey. The internists completing the survey indicated that 4.8 percent of their patients read self-help books quite often, 22.2 percent often, 55.6 percent sometimes, 15.9 percent rarely, and only 1.5 percent never. Reports of really helpful self-help works were experienced by 77.4 percent of the internists, whereas none reported them as harmful.

Another study by Starker (1988), based on a national survey of 400 randomly selected psychologists from the National Register of Health Service Providers in Psychology, found that of the 123 psychologists completing the survey, many used self-help books in their practice. The respondents reported that 60 percent of psychologists used self-help books occasionally, 24 percent often, and only 4 percent never. Starker (1986, 1988) made the following conclusions concerning his research:

1. Self-help books are widely read and prescribed by psychotherapists, particularly psychologists.

2. Mental health professionals widely read, approve of, and prescribe self-help books.

3. Mental health professionals regularly select and prescribe popular self-help titles.

4. The vast majority of self-help books used are self-selected, with only a small number prescribed by psychotherapists.

The following books, according to the research by Giblin (1989) and Starker (1988), are most commonly used in practice:

Between Parent and Child by H. Ginott

The Boys' and Girls' Book about Divorce by R. Gardner

The Cinderella Complex: Women's Hidden Fear of Independence by C. Dowling

Families: Applications of Social Learning to Families by G. Patterson

Feeling Good: The New Mood Therapy by D. Burns

How to Survive the Loss of a Love by M. Colgrove

Living with Children: New Methods for Parents and Teachers by G. Patterson and M. Gullion

On Death and Dying by E. Kubler-Ross

Male Sexuality: A Guide to Sexual Fulfillment by B. Zilbergeld

The Magic Years by S. Fraiberg

Parent Effectiveness Training by W. Becker

P.E.T.: Parent Effectiveness Training by T. Gordon

Shyness: What It Is, What to Do about It by P. Zimbardo

Your Perfect Right: A Guide to Assertive Behavior by R. Alberti and M. Emmons

What Color Is Your Parachute? by R. Bolles

When I Say No, I Feel Guilty by M. Smith

Where Did I Come From? by P. Mayle

Starker (1988) found that psychologists with a psychodynamic orientation were less inclined to prescribe self-help books like those listed above. Therapists with a cognitive-behavioral paradigm, however, were more likely to prescribe self-help books. Providing written material is now considered quite as legitimate as any other behavioral or cognitive prescription.

What does the research tell us concerning the effectiveness of self-help books? Several studies in the 1970s indicate we should use caution when implementing self-help books in treatment. First, research conducted by Zeiss (1978) suggests that techniques applied successfully by therapist are not always self-administered successfully. Zeiss conducted a controlled outcome study on the treatment of premature ejaculation. Couples were randomly assigned to receive therapist-directed treatment, self-administered treatment, and treatment with minimal therapist contact. None of the couples completing self-administered treatment successfully completed the program.

Matson and Ollendick (1977) found similar results when they evaluated the effectiveness of *Toilet Training in Less Than a Day* by Azin and Fox (1974). In this study, only one of five mothers in a self-administered group were successful; four of five mothers in therapist-directed treatment successfully toilet trained their children. Matson and Ollendick (1977) also found that behavioral problems increased in the group of children who went through the self-administered program.

Brownell, Heckerman, and Westlake (1978) found that repeated short-term losses in weight can have harmful side effects on physical health. After finding only minimal weight loss among those who used self-help books, they concluded:

In light of those potential hazards, and considering that the do-it-your-self has little medical or psychological guidance, diets designed to be self-administered should be subject to controlled clinical investigations prior to distribution, and consumers should be educated to the merits and drawbacks of specific programs. (p. 594)

The reader must keep the above quote in mind so as to help ensure that books are used appropriately in practice.

A number of studies from the 1970s suggest that self-administered programs are sometimes difficult to complete. Rosen, Glasgow, and Barrera (1976) found that a self-administered desensitization program did evidence a reduction in anxiety, but only 50 percent of the participants completed the program. Glasgow and Rosen (1978) found a similar rate of compliance in their research. However, Mahoney and Thoresen (1974) found that using a positive reward system can increase the percentage of clients completing a self-administered program.

During the 1980s a number of studies were conducted on self-help books. These generally suggest that behaviorally based readings appear to be effective. Four studies found that bibliotherapy was useful for changing inappropriate behavior of adolescents (Frankel and Merbaun, 1982; Harbaugh, 1984; Miller, 1982; Swantic, 1986). Pezzot-Pearce, LeBow, and Pearce (1982) concluded that reading a behavioral manual alone was effective in weight loss. Bailey (1982) reported that reading a self-help manual effectively treated insomnia. Rucker (1983) and Cuevas (1984) concluded that the behaviorally based self-help approach was effective in treating obesity and chronic headaches. Three studies used comparison treatment groups; one found self-help books effective in changing children's behavior (Klingman, 1985), another found them useful in improving conversation skills, and a third found them effective in weight loss (Black and Threlfall, 1986). Conner (1981) found that self-help books did not improve interpersonal skills. Galliford (1982) found no evidence for their effectiveness with weight control. Giles (1986) reported that reading stories describing reinforcement contingencies did not shape the immediate behavior of clinically troubled children. The above findings suggest that behaviorally based readings are often effective in treatment; consequently practitioners and others can use these kinds of materials with some confidence as an intervention tool.

Recent research suggests mixed results for the effectiveness of fiction as a therapeutic tool for changing one's feelings about the self. Studies by DeFrances et al. (1982) and Shafron (1983) found limited support for fiction as an effective tool for changing self-concept. However, Bohlmann (1986), Ray (1983), and Taylor (1982) all found that books were a useful tool for improving one's self-concept.

Other research concluded that fiction has a positive impact on treating sexual dysfunction (Dodge, Glasgow, and O'Neill, 1982). Ford, Bashford, and DeWitt (1984) found some support for the effectiveness of fiction in marital counseling. Finally, Morris-Vann (1983) and Sadler (1982) found fiction could be helpful for improving the emotional well-being of clients.

Pardeck and Pardeck (1984), in their review of the literature on the effectiveness of fiction as a therapeutic tool, found 24 studies supporting the positive use of books in changing attitudes of clients, increasing client assertiveness, and changing behavior of clients.

Even though there are mixed empirical findings for the effectiveness of books in treatment, nonetheless numerous clinicians use books in treatment. Riordan (1991, p. 306) summarizes the current state of using books in treatment as follows:

> Many of us find colleagues of differing orientations using articles, book chapters, poems, or other references to clarify, instruct, reinforce, or otherwise assist in therapy. The pertinent issue is not really whether bibliotherapy is effective as a separate therapy, but rather what, when, and how it should be used as part of a treatment plan.

In essence, the use of books in treatment will continue to be an important adjunct used by many therapists. Furthermore, even though it is critical to continue to conduct research on the effectiveness of bibliotherapy, the sharing of resources, of who is using what and why, and under what conditions will only add precision to the use of books in therapy (Riordan, 1991).

CONCLUSION

The use of books in treatment is apparently very common. As reported in the research, psychologists, health care professionals, and others often recommend and use books in helping people cope with problems. Evidence also suggests that many lay persons use self-help books to deal with issues related to personal growth and development. Even though the verdict is still out on the effectiveness of books in treatment, there is little to suggest that the popularity of bibliotherapy among professionals and lay persons will abate. A number of psychologists have reacted to this current situation with alarm. However, it would be very difficult to regulate what is produced by the self-help book industry in a free society. What is important, however, is that consumers of self-help books and related reading materials realize the limitations of bibliotherapy and that it is not a cure-all for problems. Therapists in turn should use books in treatment in a reasonable fashion and continue to report the effectiveness of bibliotherapy in practice to the professional community. Starker (1988) also suggests that therapists who use a cognitive-behavioral treatment style of intervention will more likely be comfortable using self-help books. Those therapists who use a psychodynamic orientation are more likely to feel comfortable with the use of fiction in treatment. One must keep in mind that the use of nonfiction versus fiction has more empirical support in the research literature.

Even though books as a treatment tool are widely used by both professionals and lay persons, one must be aware of the limitations of this approach. Rubin (1978) concludes that the critical issue of books in treatment is not necessarily what books do to people but rather what they do to reading books. In other words, a reader may develop unrealistic expectations about solving a problem through a self-help book because the person does not know the limitations of bibliotherapy. Furthermore, the reader may misinterpret, noncomply, project into, or otherwise misuse books, and so avoid responsibility for a problem (Giblin, 1989).

Therapists should be particularly aware that if books are introduced in treatment at an inappropriate time, they will lessen the chances for successful outcome. It is best that bibliotherapy be implemented only after an appropriate relationship is established between client and therapist. Obviously, if a client is moving toward a speedy resolution of a presenting problem, there is little need for books in treatment. It should also be realized that books should not be employed as a single helping strategy but should be seen largely as an adjunct to treatment.

One of the most critical issues relating to books in treatment, both self-help and fiction, is that the client should be in the habit of reading; this is especially important in using bibliotherapy with children. However, it should be realized that many books are on audio tape; thus the problem of the nonreader is less critical if a book is in an audio format. However, bibliotherapeutic techniques have generally been found most effective with clients whose reading abilities are average or above (Zaccaria and Moses, 1968). The therapist must also be aware of the reading and interest levels of the client, regardless of age. Reading that does not interest the client will not be effective. A book that is too difficult may frustrate the client and even intensify the problem. A final limitation of books in treatment is that the therapist must be sure that reading, versus other factors, is impacting change in the person being helped. What this means is the therapist may mistakenly use books as a treatment tool with future clients, when in fact earlier successes were due to other factors.

Finally, professionals and lay persons should keep the above points in mind when using books as a tool for solving problems. If the limitations of self-help books and fiction are understood, the benefits of the bibliotherapeutic process can be realized by all who use books as a tool to deal with problems.

REFERENCES

Azin, N. H., and R. M. Fox (1974). *Toilet training in less than a day*. New York: Simon & Schuster.

Bailey, C. A. (1982). Effects of therapist contact and a self-help manual in the treatment of sleep-onset insomnia. *Dissertation Abstracts International*, 43, 2022A.

Barker, R. L. (1987). *The social work dictionary*. Silver Springs, MD: NASW.

Berne, E. (1964). *Games people play*. New York: Grove Press.

Bernstein, J. (1989). *Bibliotherapy: How books can help children cope*. In *Children's literature: Resource for the classroom*, ed. M. Rudman, 159–173. New York: Christopher Gordon Publishers, Inc.

Berry, I. (1978). Contemporary bibliotherapy: Systematizing the field. In *Bibliotherapy Sourcebook*, ed. E. J. Rubin, 185-190. Phoenix, AZ: Oryx Press.

Black, D. R., and W. E. Threlfall (1986). A stepped approach to weight control: A minimal intervention and a bibliotherapy problem-solving program. *Behavior Therapy*, 17, 144–157.

Bohlmann, N. R. (1986). Use of RET bibliotherapy to increase self-acceptance and self-actualization levels of runners. *Dissertation Abstracts International*, 46, 2191A (University Microfilms No. 85-23, 265).

Brownell, K. D., C. L. Heckerman, and R. J. Westlake (1978). Therapist and group contact as variables in the behavioral treatment of obesity. *Behaviour Research and Therapy*, 16, 323–333.

Carnegie, D. (1936). *How to win friends and influence people*. New York: Pocket Books.

Conner, C. N. (1981). The effectiveness of bibliotherapy on teaching initiator dating skills to females. *Dissertation Abstracts International*, 42, 3818B (University Microfilms No. 82-03, 109).

Cuevas, J. L. (1984). Cognitive treatment of chronic tension headache. *Dissertation Abstracts International*, 46, 955B (University Microfilms No. 85-10, 012).

DeFrances, J., K. Dexter, T. J. Leary, and J. R. MacMullen (1982). The effect of bibliotherapy and videotaping techniques on collective and self-concept formation in behaviorally disordered youth. *Proceedings of the 60th Annual International Convention of the Council for Exceptional Children*. Houston, TX (ERIC Document Reproduction Service No. ED 218 885).

Dodge, L. T., R. E. Glasgow, and H. K. O'Neill (1982). Bibliotherapy in the treatment of female orgasmic dysfunction. *Journal of Consulting & Clinical Psychology*, 50, 442–443.

Ford, J. D., M B. Bashford, and K. N. DeWitt (1984). Three approaches to marital enrichment: Toward optimal matching of participants and interventions. *Journal of Sex & Marital Therapy*, 10, 41–48.

Frankel, M. J., and M. Merbaum (1982). Effects of therapist contact and a self-control manual on nailbiting reduction. *Behavior Therapy*, 13, 125–129.

Galliford, J. E. (1982). Eliminating self-defeating behavior: The effects of ESDB bibliotherapy compared to ESDB group therapy on weight control in women. *Dissertation Abstracts International*, 43, 1978B (University Microfilms No. 82-24, 784).

Giblin, P. (1989). Use of reading assignments in clinical practice. *The American Journal of Family Therapy*, 17, 219–228.

Giles, L. P. (1986) Effects of reading-mediated vicarious reinforcement on the behavior of disturbed children. *Dissertation Abstracts International*, 47, 4299B (University Microfilms No. 87-02, 267).

Glasgow, R. E., and G. M. Rosen (1978). Behavioral bibliotherapy: A review of self-help behavior therapy manuals. *Psychological Bulletin*, 85(1), 1–23.

Glasgow, R. E., and G. M. Rosen (1979). Self-help behavior therapy manuals: Recent developments and clinical usage. *Clinical Behavior Therapy Review*, 1, 1–20.

Goldiamond, I. (1976). Singling out self-administered behavior therapies for professional review. *American Psychologist*, 31, 142–147.

Harbaugh, J. K. (1984). The effectiveness of bibliotherapy in teaching problem solving skills to female juvenile delinquents. *Dissertation Abstracts International*, 45, 3072A (University Microfilms No. 84-29, 693).

Harris, T. A. (1968). *I'm O.K.–you're O.K.* New York: Harper and Row.

Katz, B., and L. Sternberg Katz (1985). *Self-help: 1400 best books on personal growth*. New York: R. R. Bowker Co.

Klingman, A. (1985). Responding to a bereaved classmate: Comparison of two strategies for death education in the classroom. *Death Studies*, 9, 449–454.

Mahoney, M. J., and C. E. Thoresen (1974). *Self-control: Power to the person*. Monterey, CA: Brooks Cole.

Matson, M. J., and T. H. Ollendick (1977). Issues in toilet training normal children. *Behavior Therapy*, 8, 549–553.

Menninger, K. A. (1945). *The human mind*. New York: A. A. Knopf.

Miller, D. L. (1982). Effect of a program of therapeutic discipline on the attitude, attendance, and insight of truant adolescents. *Dissertation Abstracts International*, 43, 1048A (University Microfilms No. 82-20, 323).

Morris-Vann, A. M. (1983). The efficacy of bibliotherapy on the mental health of elementary students who have experienced a loss precipitated by parental unemployment, divorce, marital separation or death. *Dissertation Abstracts International*, 44, 676A (University Microfilms No. 83-15, 616).

Pardeck, J. A., and J. T. Pardeck (1984). *Young people with problems: A guide to bibliotherapy*. Westport, CT: Greenwood Press.

Pardeck, J. T. (1992). Using bibliotherapy in treatment with children in residential care. *Residential Treatment for Children and Youth*, 9, 73–90.

Pardeck, J. T., and J. A. Pardeck (1987). Using bibliotherapy to help children cope with the changing family. *Social Work in Education*, 9, 107–116.

Pezzot-Pearce, T. D., M. D. LeBow, and J. W. Pearce (1982). Increasing cost-effectiveness in obesity treatment through use of self-help behavioral manuals and decreased therapist contact. *Journal of Consulting & Clinical Psychology*, 50, 448–449.

Ray, R. D. (1983). The relationship of bibliotherapy, self-concept and reading readiness among kindergarten children. *Dissertation Abstracts International*, 45, 140A (University Microfilms No. 84-02, 425).

Riordan, R. J. (1991). Bibliotherapy revisited. *Psychological Reports*, 68, 306.

Rosen, G. M. (1976). The development and use of nonprescription behavior therapies. *American Psychologist*, 31, 139–141.

Rosen, G. M. (1981). Guidelines for the review of do-it-yourself books. *Contemporary Psychology*, 26, 189–91.

Rosen, G. M., R. E. Glasgow, and M. A. Barrera (1976). Controlled study to assess the clinical efficacy of totally self-administered systematic desensitization. *Journal of Consulting and Clinical Psychology*, 44, 208–217.

Rubin, R. (1978). *Using bibliotherapy: A guide to theory and practice*. Phoenix, AZ: Oryx Press.

Rucker, J. P. (1983). An outcome study of two short-term weight loss methods: Bibliotherapy and interpersonal growth group therapy. *Dissertation Abstracts International*, 44, 2421A.

Sadler, M. S. (1982). The effects of bibliotherapy on anomie and life satisfaction of the elderly. *Literature, Literary Response, and the Teaching of Literature.* Abstracts of doctoral dissertations published in *Dissertation Abstracts International, January through June 1983* (vol. 43, nos. 7–12) (ERIC Document Reproduction Service No. ED 230 983).

Savage, S. A., C. R. Hollin, and A. J. Hayward (1990). Self-help manuals for problem drinking: The relative effects of their educational and therapeutic components. *British Journal of Clinical Psychology, 29,* 373–382.

Shafron, P. W. (1983). Relationship between bibliotherapy and the self-esteem of junior high school students enrolled in remedial reading classes. *Dissertation Abstracts International,* 44, 1037A (University Microfilms No. 83-18, 314).

Spock, B. (1946). *The pocket book of baby and child care.* New York: Pocket Books.

Starker, S. (1986). Promises and prescriptions: Self-help books in mental health and medicine. *American Journal of Health Promotion,* 1, 19–24 and 68.

Starker, S. (1988). Psychologists and self-help books: Attitudes and prescriptive practices of clinicians. *American Journal of Psychotherapy,* 42, 448–455.

Swantic, F. M. (1986). An investigation of the effectiveness of bibliotherapy on middle grade students who repeatedly display inappropriate behavior in the school setting. *Dissertation Abstracts International,* 47, 843A.

Taylor, V. W. (1982). An investigation of the effect of bibliotherapy on the self-concepts of kindergarten children from one-parent families. *Dissertation Abstracts International,* 43, 3505A (University Microfilms No. 83-06, 465).

Webster's New Collegiate Dictionary (1985). Springfield, MA: Merriam-Webster.

Zaccaria, J., and H. Moses (1968). *Facilitating human development through reading: The use of bibliotherapy in teaching and counseling.* Champaign, IL: Stipes.

Zeiss, R. A. (1978). *Prolong your pleasure.* New York: Pocket Books.

2

Clinical Applications

Glasgow and Rosen (1978, 1979) offered one of the first detailed reviews of the self-help book literature. The work of Craighead, McNamara, and Horan (1984, p. 880) helped to define the many uses of self-help books in treatment by building on Glasgow and Rosen's work. These include the following strategies for using books in treatment:

1. *Self-administered* refers to conditions in which the client receives a book or other written material, and has no other contact with the therapist beyond the initial and post-test assessment sessions. This is often referred to as a no contact approach.

2. *Minimal-contact* refers to conditions in which the client relies primarily on the written material but may have some contact with the therapist. This contact is in the form of written correspondence, phone calls, or meetings.

3. *Therapist-administered* is a strategy where the client receives the written material but also meets regularly with the therapist. These meetings include discussing the material and implementing procedures to bring about change. This form of intervention may be conducted in individual or group sessions.

4. *Therapist-directed* consists of the traditional weekly interview that calls for the therapist to be actively involved in the client's treatment. A typical strategy is to use self-monitoring or homework assignments between therapy session.

Craighead, McNamara, and Horan (1984) conclude that there are three types of self-help books. One is the *self-help manual*, written with the intent to help the troubled individual. This kind of self-help book is bought over the counter and is often implemented without necessarily consulting a therapist.

In contrast, the *participant* or *student manual* demands that the therapist have some kind of involvement. This kind of manual often has self-monitoring forms, exercises, and summaries of specific procedures. The manual is best described as an adjunct to traditional treatment.

The *leader* or *therapist manual* is one step removed from the traditional self-help book. It is designed to train therapists to help clients implement a particular procedure or program. The assumption is that the client is not able to understand or implement the treatment program on his or her own. In turn, the trained therapist must be a part of the treatment program for it to be successful. Presently, there are few participant or leader manuals available. Most self-help books are designed to be self-administered or as an adjunct to treatment.

No specific model of self-help has emerged. Craighead, McNamara, and Horan (1984) offer a general model for self-help intervention through books.

1. Specific techniques offered in the book are the primary ingredient of client change or the therapeutic relationship.

2. The techniques offered in the book must be in language the client can understand.

3. The techniques offered must be standardized; that is, they are applicable to many people, not simply one.

4. The technique must have a relatively low risk level.

5. The individual is considered capable of selecting and has the right to select the goals of treatment, as opposed to an expert.

6. Individuals are considered to be capable of self-instructed change.

What this general model suggests is that people should be empowered to make decisions about their own lives. Furthermore, one might argue that the model is grounded in two scientific theories, specifically behavioral and cognitive theories.

Skinner (1953) speculated that individuals have the ability to control their own behavior. In the behavioral theoretical tradition, individual behavior is largely determined by external factors. Homme's (1965) cognitive view suggests that "operants of the mind" trigger attempts to extend self-control procedures to include changes in thoughts as well as behavior. Self-help books are well grounded in the behavioral and cognitive theoretical traditions. Virtually all self-help books emphasize changing or modifying one's environment if the problem is triggered by environmental forces. Also offered in many self-help programs are self-monitoring exercises, self-evaluation, and self-reinforcements. All strategies are well grounded in behavioral and cognitive theoretical traditions.

Mahoney and Thoresen (1974) have even argued that self-help books are more effective than traditional therapies. They argue that greater behavioral change is possible if self-promoted. In fact, the role of the therapist is simply to empower the client through self-help books. The control of treatment thus shifts from the therapist to the client. Even though Mahoney and Thoresen are largely speculating about the role of self-help books in treatment, more research should be conducted on the effectiveness of self-help books versus traditional therapies.

SELF-HELP BOOKS IN TREATMENT

A number of strategies can be used to ensure the effectiveness of self-help books. The use of these various strategies is largely determined by how a self-help book is utilized in treatment.

Timing

When a self-help book is offered as part of the treatment process is critical to successful outcome. The therapist should do careful preparation and planning before offering a self-help book to a client. It is critical for the client to have choices in determining what titles will be used. A self-help book should never be forced upon the client like medicine but rather as a resource of empowerment. The client must be ready and willing to use the book in treatment.

For example, when grieving is at its peak, it is difficult for individuals to face their emotions. The presenting problem is known to the client, and emotional relief is first needed in other areas of social functioning. Until the client is ready, it is very difficult to confront the grief directly. In fact, if a therapist is not sensitive to the issue of timing and a book is introduced at the wrong time, the client's fears, guilt, and depression may be intensified through the self-help book.

Discussion

In treatment, a self-help book must first be read before it is discussed. It should be noted, however, that a great deal can be learned by simply reading the self-help book without discussing it with anyone.

If the book is used in treatment, one of the most important aspects of discussion is that the therapist should be a good listener. It is critical for the therapist to listen with empathy. This allows the client to have maximum opportunity to express feelings about a problem. This process also enhances trust between the therapist and client. As has been well documented in successful therapy, trust, respect, and empathy are all critical components of successful therapy (Rogers, 1969).

Preparation

Prior to implementing a self-help book in treatment, Bernstein (1989) concludes that a number of factors need to be considered about the book. The first, which seems obvious, is that the therapist should first read the book. Other critical steps to preparation include:

1. What is the scope of the self-help book?

2. Is the book accurate, or is there information that must be clarified or corrected?

3. Will the book have an emotional impact?

4. What is the religious or moral perspective of the book?

5. Is the self-help book worthwhile from a literary viewpoint; this is, will it satisfy the readers on an emotional and verbal level, and possibly on a spiritual level?

6. Is the book fiction or nonfiction, or is it propaganda?

7. Is the self-help book appropriate for the person's age, interests, and reading level?

8. Will the self-help book's length, format, or level of difficulty impede any clinical gains?

9. Is the self-help book in keeping with the audience's general developmental life tasks, such as someone entering marriage or having a first child?

10. Does the client have special needs; that is, does he or she need large-print or an audio book, or does the client have a low vocabulary, which means sensitivity to the reading level of the book?

By thoroughly exploring the above issues, the therapist will have a chance of success in using self-help books in treatment. Individuals who use books in a self-administered approach can also use these guidelines to explore the quality of a given self-help book.

CRITICAL ISSUES

The popularization of self-help books and the prediction of an increased role of books in treatment (Pardeck, 1992) are critical issues that should be explored before introducing books in treatment. These specifically deal with the negative effects of self-help approaches.

Becvar (1978) suggests that self-help books tend to offer a liberal definition of mental illness. Individuals experiencing normal developmental issues may come to label these as mental illness, thus exacerbating issues. Self-help books have a tendency to offer utopian solutions that may well set unrealistic expectations for what is positive mental health. Such a situation only contributes to further dissatisfaction and unhappiness.

Therapists should also be sensitive to ineffective programs. This is obviously a major concerns for individuals who are deciding on a self-administered program. Even though consumers have a right to choose, unfortunately they may lack the needed information to choose wisely. Ineffective programs may erode consumer confidence in self-help books and may ultimately affect the trust levels of professional practitioners. A related problem to that of ineffective self-help books is they may actually exacerbate the client's problem. It is critical for therapists and consumers to study clearly the claims made by a self-help book program. If a consumer cannot make an appropriate judgment about the quality of a self-help book program, he or she should ask a professional about the effectiveness of a given self-help program.

The final concern for therapists and those who use self-administered programs is the problem of inappropriate self-diagnosis. When using a self-administered program, the reader must determine both the type and severity of a problem. An inaccurate self-diagnosis may cause a person to choose a self-administered program, when in reality a more intensive approach is needed. The best solution to this potential problem is for therapists to provide the needed assistance to clients at all stages of a self-help program. Consumers of self-help books must carefully choose an appropriate self-help program and seek professional guidance if they are not sure about its appropriate use.

Goldiamond (1976) concludes that there are many ethical issues related to self-help books. These need to be considered carefully by the therapist, and consumers should also be aware of them. Finally, self-help programs appear to be within the ethical standards of most helping professions as long as they have an education-training context or personal advice from a professional who is a licensed therapist.

EXAMPLES OF SELF-HELP BOOKS

There are numerous self-help books available for dealing with problems ranging from improving parenting to recovering from addiction. The following examples of self-help books deal with issues relating to parenting and addiction.

You Are Your Child's First Teacher by Baldwin (1989) is aimed at supporting parents during the early childhood years. Baldwin argues that parents are the most important teachers during this critical period of growth and development. The book covers the following topics:

1. Parent as the child's first teacher

2. Receiving and care for the newborn

3. Growth and development

4. A baby's development during the first year

5. Helping toddlers develop

6. Parenting issues during the first three years

7. Fantasy and creative play

8. Self-imagination

9. Artistic ability

10. Musical ability

11. Discipline

12. Cognitive development

Baldwin (1989) points out that parents receive contradictory information about all of the above topics. She attempts to provide new ways of seeing and understanding children, *not* a set of rules for raising children.

Under the topic of parents as first teachers, for example, Baldwin (1989) explores the cultural dilemmas related to parenting and the changing family. Baldwin stresses that children are not tiny adults and that parents should trust their own judgments about parenting. Also offered are information on how children learn and a detailed reading list.

As found under the topic of parents as first teachers, Baldwin offers detailed information focusing on skills and insight for each topic covered. Baldwin's book can serve as a guide for a parent simply seeking information about child development. One might also use her work as the central manual for a parenting group wishing to improve their parenting skills. Using the self-help book approach proposed by Craighead, McNamara, and Horan (1984), *You Are Your Child's First Teacher* can be viewed as a self-administered manual for improving parenting skills, as well as a text that might serve as a useful adjunct to treatment with a parent working closely with a practitioner. Thus, a practitioner may recommend the work simply as a book read on one's own or as an intricate part of treatment.

Recovery from Addiction (Finnegan and Gray, 1990) presents a comprehensive survey of the numerous factors involved in creating and healing the addictive or alcoholic condition. The work explores the social, economic, and political involvement, as well as the spiritual and psychological dimensions of codependency and addiction. The primary focus of *Recovery from Addiction* is on effective nutritional and medical therapies that help correct the biochemical disorders that are the basis of addictions.

As a self-help book, *Recovery from Addiction* includes a 12–step program that the authors claim is the most successful recovery program to date. The authors include chapters on getting help, types of addiction, codependency, and diet. Under the chapters dealing with diet, nutritional therapies and recipes are offered. The authors conclude that nutritional therapy is critical for one to achieve a real and lasting recovery from addition. They suggest that the main requirements of a nutritional program include:

1. It must be effective.

2. It must be practical and easy to implement.

3. It must be relatively inexpensive.

According to *Recovery from Addiction*, the cornerstones of nutritional support are formulas that strengthen metabolism, increase energy, and heighten one's overall sense of well-being. Finnegan and Gray conclude that clients can break free of addiction within a short time period after implementing a careful diet. In their book, they offer a recovery program for addicts, as well as approaches for strengthening codependents who have weakened their health. The following formulas are included:

1. Concentrate foods

2. Whole food extracts

3. Whole food herbs and medicinal herbs and formulas

4. Minerals

5. Amino acids

6. Vitamins

7. Beneficial digestive floras

8. Enzymes

Diets offered in the book include the above formulas. Finnegan and Gray recommend that the recovering addict work closely with a physician when implementing the diet program.

Finnegan and Gray's (1990) *Recovery from Addiction* might be used as a self-administered program or as an adjunct to therapy for the recovering addict. What is interesting about their approach is that they do recognize what sociologists and humanitarians have suggested for a number of years: alcoholics and addicts are often victims of nonsupportive environments, poverty, poor education, lack of job opportunities, exploitative and oppressive economic and political conditions, and other problems related to the social environment. They conclude that these are essential factors that must be dealt with; however, they are not the whole picture. The purpose of their self-help book is *not* to focus on environmental factors but rather to focus on the metabolic causes of addiction that they feel can be corrected through nutritional therapies.

Healing the Addictive Mind (Jampolsky, 1991) offers approaches for freeing one's self from addictive patterns and relationships. The author suggests that the human conditions that affect most people, fixed in habits of thinking that keep one stuck, can be corrected by focusing on the following issues:

1. The fallacy of looking outside of ourselves.

2. The structure of the addictive thought system.

3. The core beliefs of the addictive thought system.

4. The structure of the love-based thought system.

5. The core beliefs of the love-based thought system.

6. Addiction and the fear of intimacy.

7. Learning to love ourselves.

8. Growing as a couple.

A core goal of the book is to illustrate to the reader through the above topics that addictive behavior is *not* limited to a reliance on alcohol or other drugs; instead, addiction to chemical substances is a metaphor for one's current social condition. Jampolsky argues that the roots of addiction lie not in a bottle but in one's search for happiness. The goal of his work is to help one achieve peace of mind.

An example of the self-help techniques that Jampolsky offers can be found under the topic of core beliefs of the addictive thought system. He suggests that the addictive mind becomes bitterly entrenched in this belief system, leaving one devoid of love or serenity. These beliefs include some of the following:

1. I am alone in a cruel, harsh, and unforgiving world. I am separate from everyone else.

2. If I want safety and peace of mind, I must judge others and be quick to defend myself.

3. My way is the right way. My perceptions are always factually correct. In order to feel good about myself, I need to be perfect all of the time.

4. Attack and defense are my only safety.

In order to change one's negative thought system, Jampolsky recommends that one needs to change negative thoughts by focusing on beliefs that bring peace of mind. These include:

1. What I see in others is a reflection of my own state of mind. There is an underlying unity to all life. I lack nothing to be happy and whole right now.

2. My safety lies in my defenselessness, because love needs no defense. Acceptance is what brings me peace of mind.

3. My self-worth is not based upon my performance. Love is unconditional.

4. Forgiveness, with no exceptions, ensures peace.

The author concludes that using positive thoughts alone does not necessarily bring about change. One must also identify the negative beliefs–the addictive beliefs–that keep one from being able to embrace the truth. Thus, if one finds the self in conflict, one's first task is to identify the addictive belief. The second task is to replace it with love-based thinking.

The final section of *Healing the Addictive Mind* offers Daily Lessons. These lessons provide a framework and exercises for better understanding the cycles of addiction and how peace of mind is always a possible alternative. The Daily Lessons are designed to provide a practical means for living a life free of addiction and to help one remove the blocks to the awareness of love. Like the other self-help books overviewed in this chapter, *Healing the Addictive Mind* can be used as a self-administered treatment program or as an adjunct to therapy.

CONCLUSION

The use of self-help books in clinical practice is extensive among helping professionals. Research by Starker (1988) concludes that the general population has an expanding interest in self-help books. A typical self-help program uses written materials, self-monitoring, information giving, and positive reinforcement.

As pointed out in this chapter, self-help books can be used in four ways: *self-administered* with no therapist contact; *minimal contact* using a clinician as a guide to the use of the book; *clinical-administered* where the client receives the book at beginning of therapy followed by regular meetings with the therapist; and *clinician-directed* with traditional weekly treatment and a major focus on the self-help materials (Pardeck, 1992).

The following observations by Starker (1988) provide insight into the use of self-help books in practice. These points will also be useful to the consumer of self-help programs:

1. Consumers purchase self-help books in vast quantities and largely feel they are often helpful.

2. Clinicians are generally positive about self-help books and often prescribe them to clients.

3. Self-help books are usually written in response to a current social problem and, consequently, may be viewed as a factor in promoting social change.

4. Self-help books that do not prescribe specific behavioral procedures to achieve clinical change are not readily evaluated in an empirical sense.

5. Self-help books offering specific cures or treatment for clinical problems are often capable of being evaluated; however, the process of evaluation is imprecise and will likely not have an impact on the producers of self-help books.

6. Self-help books will continue to be popular among readers and many clinicians, even though these books often lack empirical validation.

Finally, even though the research evidence offers mixed findings on the effectiveness of self-help books, it has not proven that they are not helpful. Given this condition, therapists and consumers of self-helps should use them with some degree of caution. The clinical applications of self-help books are extensive if one keeps in mind the strategies useful to applying them to practice, their limitations as suggested by the research findings, and the need for more empirical testing of self-help programs.

REFERENCES

Baldwin, R. (1989). *You are your child's first teacher*. Berkeley, CA: Celestial Arts.

Becvar, R. J. (1978). Self-help books: Some ethical questions. *Personnel and Guidance Journal, 57*, 160–162.

Bernstein, J. (1989). Bibliotherapy: How books can help children cope. In *Children's literature: Resource for the classroom*, ed. M. Rudman, 159–173. New York: Christopher Gordon Publishers, Inc.

Craighead, L., K. McNamara, and J. Horan (1984). Perspectives on self-help and bibliotherapy: You are what you read. In *Handbook of counseling psychology*, ed. S. Brown and R. Lent, 878–929. New York: John Wiley and Sons.

Finnegan, J., and D. Gray (1990). *Recovery from addiction*. Berkeley, CA: Celestial Arts.

Glasgow, R. E., and G. M. Rosen (1978). Behavioral bibliotherapy: A review of self-help behavior therapy manuals. *Psychological Bulletin, 85*(1), 1–23.

Glasgow, R. E., and G. M. Rosen (1979). Self-help behavior therapy manuals: Recent developments and clinical usage. *Clinical Behavior Therapy Review,* 1, 1–20.

Goldiamond, I. (1976). Singling out self-administered behavior therapies for professional review. *American Psychologist,* 31, 142–147.

Homme, L. E. (1965). Perspectives in psychology, XXIV: Control of coverants, the operants of the mind. *Psychological Record,* 15, 501–511.

Jampolsky, L. (1991). *Healing the addictive mind.* Berkeley, CA: Celestial Arts.

Mahoney, M. J., and C. E. Thoresen (1974). *Self-control: Power to the person.* Monterey, CA: Brooks/Cole.

Pardeck, J. T. (1992). Using bibliotherapy in treatment with children in residential care. *Residential Treatment for Children and Youth,* 9, 73–90.

Rogers, C. (1969). *Freedom to learn.* Columbus, OH: Charles E. Merrill.

Skinner, B. F. (1953). *Science and human behavior.* New York: The Free Press.

Starker, S. (1988). Psychologists and self-help books: Attitudes and prescriptive practices of clinicians. *American Journal of Psychotherapy,* 42, 448–455.

3

Chemical Dependency

Chemical dependency is probably best understood as an adaptive behavior by an individual embedded within a troubled family system. Numerous theorists increasingly agree with this position as an explanation for why family members abuse alcohol as well as other drugs (Bateson et al., 1956; Haley, 1973; Jackson, 1957; Wegcheider, 1981). Clearly there is growing recognition (Ben-Yehuda and Schindell, 1981; Stanton, 1978; Wilson and Oxford, 1978) that the family system is critical to the initiation, maintenance, cessation, and prevention of alcohol and drug use by one or more family members.

A family systems approach suggests that individuals who abuse chemicals are significantly connected (developmentally and physically) to their family. Their behavior is tightly bound up with various family pressures; when persons push for individuation and separation within the chemically dependent family system, the family resists the change. These codependent family systems attempt to retard or postpone the process of individuation, which results in dysfunctional family alignments. Children from chemically dependent systems may continue these patterns of behavior into their 20s, 30s, and beyond (Vaillant, 1966). Brake estimates that one in five children lives in an alcoholic family; thus, the lives of approximately eight million children revolve around alcohol. Wilson and Blocher (1990) conclude that sons of alcoholic fathers are five times more likely to become alcoholics, and daughters of alcoholic mothers are three times more likely to become alcoholics than girls from nonalcoholic family systems.

A number of theorists maintain that chemical dependency is a family-based problem that affects and involves all family members (Brake, 1988; Weddle and Wilson, 1986; Wegscheider, 1981; Wilson and Oxford, 1978). The characteristics of chemically dependent families are indicative of families affected by alcohol and drug abuse.

Chemically dependent families tend to have rules that contribute to dysfunctional behaviors. One rule is that the person affected by chemicals is the most important aspect of the family's life. The dependent person's top priority is abusing chemicals, whereas the family's priority is the dependent person and attempting to keep chemicals away from that person. Obviously, the priorities of the chemically dependent person and the family are in conflict.

Denial is also common in the chemically dependent family system. Family members do not see the drug or alcohol as the cause of the problem. Another rule is that the dependent person is not responsible for his or her behavior, a position that makes individual behavioral change difficult in the dysfunctional family system. Often someone else is blamed for the person's behavior; thus, reality testing in the chemically dependent family system is faulty. Family members in turn resist changing and feel more comfortable with the dependent family member abusing drugs because this behavior maintains the dysfunctional family system. Unwritten rules also forbid talking about the chemical abuse, and like closed family systems in general, members resist outside intervention and treatment.

A number of roles are also found within these dysfunctional family systems. These include the scapegoat, family hero, the mascot, and the lost child. Each of these roles is designed to protect the chemically dependent person from taking responsibility for the self. Thus, the person's drinking or drug abuse is actually reinforced by these dysfunctional roles.

The scapegoat role is often played by a member within the chemically dependent system. Even though the chemical abuse is real, there is denial by family members. This denial results in blaming someone else for family problems: the scapegoat. The scapegoat may act in negative ways to ensure the blame is appropriate. The behavior might include running away, becoming ill, or generally acting out. The role of the scapegoat is to redirect attention from the chemically dependent person to the scapegoat. Thus, family dysfunction is maintained, and problems do not have to be addressed.

In the chemically dependent system, a positive influence is needed to correct the negative behaviors of the dependent person. The family hero plays this positive role. This person is often the ideal person who does everything well and attempts to make the family function in a more positive fashion. The hero role provides the family with self-worth.

The mascot role is the person who has a good sense of humor and attempts to make serious issues not so serious. Even though this person is deeply troubled inside, he or she attempts to make family life more pleasant by providing a sense of humor. Like the other roles, the mascot role maintains the dysfunctional family.

Another role is the lost child. This individual is not involved in the family; that is, he or she simply withdraws from the family and, in turn, never causes any problems for other family members. This person requires little from the family and contributes little to the family dysfunction.

The roles of the chemically dependent family are aligned with the dysfunctional aspects of the family system. All family members suffer from the chemical dependency, and each member assumes one of these roles to maintain the dysfunctional aspects of the family. In order for the family to change, these roles must change. This is a major goal of family treatment.

Treatment of the chemically dependent family system involves each family member taking responsibility for his or her own behavior, in particular, the chemically dependent person must recognize that he or she has a problem. Thus, overcoming denial by all family members is a major goal that must be dealt with in treatment.

Family members must also understand how they contribute to the problem. They must learn to evaluate how their individual behavior maintains the dysfunctional chemically dependent family. They must be taught to confront and change their own behavior, and also to confront the chemically dependent person with honest information about his or her behavior.

Factual information on the progression of chemical dependency is also critical for family members to change. There are clear cycles to the dependency process that must be stopped, and all family members are involved in this process. If the process is not altered, the chemically dependent person will grow worse, and the family will become more dysfunctional. Numerous self-help groups are available for both family members of chemically dependent families and dependent persons.

There are many excellent self-help books that can assist family members and the chemically dependent person in gaining insight into the problems related to alcohol and chemical dependency. These include the issues related to codependency, children of alcoholics, teaching children about chemical dependency, and the neurochemical aspects of dependency. These titles can be used as self-administered programs as part of one's recovery, as titles recommended by therapists to the dependent person and his or her family, or as part of a self-help group effort for those attempting to achieve recovery.

REFERENCES

Bateson, G., D. Jackson, J. Haley, and J. Weakland (1956). Toward a theory of schizophrenia. *Behavioral Science*, 1, 251–264.

Ben-Yehuda, N., and B. Schindell (1981). The addict's family origin: An empirical survey analysis. *International Journal of the Addictions*, 16, 273–282.

Brake, K. (1988). Counseling young children of alcoholics. *Elementary School Guidance and Counseling*, 23, 106–111.

Haley, J. (1973). *Uncommon therapy*. New York: W. W. Norton.

Jackson, D. (1957). The question of family homeostasis. *Psychiatric Quarterly Supplement*, Part 1, 31, 79–90.

Stanton, M. (1978) The family and drug misuse: A bibliography. *American Journal of Drug and Alcohol Abuse*, 5, 151–170.

Vaillant, G. (1966). Twelve-year follow-up of New York narcotic addicts: The relation of treatment to outcome. *American Journal of Psychiatry*, 122, 727–737.

Weddle, C., and P. Wilson (1986). Children of alcoholics: What we should know; how we can help. *Children Today*, January–February, 8–12.

Wegscheider, S. (1981). *Another chance: Hope and health for the alcoholic family*. Palo Alto, CA: Science and Behavior Books.

Wilson, C., and J. Oxford (1978). Children of alcoholics: A report of preliminary study and comments on literature. *Journal of Studies on Alcohol*, 39, 121–142.

Wilson, J., and L. Blocher (1990). The counselor's role in assisting children of alcoholics. *Elementary School Guidance and Counseling*, 25, 98–106.

BOOKS ON CHEMICAL DEPENDENCY

1. Ackerman, Robert J. *Growing in the Shadow: Children of Alcoholics*. Deerfield Beach, FL: Health Communications, Inc., 1986.

    This work covers the world of children of alcoholics. The wisdom of 21 leading authorities in the field of children of alcoholics is covered in this work.

2. Ackerman, Robert J. *Let Go and Grow: Recovery for Adult Children*. Deerfield Beach, FL: Health Communications, Inc., 1987.

    This book describes the varying and diverse characteristics of adult children of alcoholics. Identified are the positive characteristics and problems areas of children of alcoholics.

3. Ackerman, Robert J., and Judith A. Michaels. *Recovery Resource Guide* (4th ed.). Deerfield Beach, FL: Health Communications, Inc., 1989.

    This work is designed for professionals and laypersons who need information on children of alcoholics, family and codependence, personal recovery, and helping agencies. The authors list over 1,000 resources that are available for recovery.

4. Alcoholics Anonymous World Services. *Alcoholics Anonymous: "The Big Book"* (3rd ed.). New York: AA World Services, 1976.

    This offers a step-by-step guide to recovery from alcoholism. These steps are aimed at achieving sobriety and serenity from the disease of alcoholism.

5. Allison, Patricia, and Jack Yost. *Hooked, but Not Helpless: Ending Your Love Hate Relationship with Nicotine*. New York: Bridge City Books, 1990.

    This is a book for those addicted to nicotine. Strategies are offered for helping people stop smoking without losing emotional balance or gaining weight.

6. Andre, Pierre. *Drug Addiction: Learn about It Before Your Kids Do*. Deerfield Beach, FL: Health Communications, Inc., 1987.

    This work takes a specialized focus on cocaine. Explored is the problem of addiction and how it takes hold of its victims. Topics included in the work cover intervention, hospitalization, and treatment follow-up.

7. Anonymous. *Chemically Dependent.* Minneapolis, MN: CompCare, 1989.
    This work offers the Chemically Dependent Anonymous (CDA) philosophy of recovery. The belief is that the addictive-compulsive use of chemicals is the core of the disease and that use of any mood-changing chemical will result in relapse.

8. Anonymous. *Narcotics Anonymous.* Minneapolis: MN: CompCare, 1989.
    This is the basic text of the Fellowship of Narcotics Anonymous. Material for this book is drawn from the personal experiences of addicts seeking support and recovery.

9. Balis, Susan Adlin. *Beyond the Illusion: Choices for Children of Alcoholics.* Deerfield Beach, FL: Health Communications, Inc., 1989.
    According to the author, children who grow up with an alcoholic parent exist in a world of illusion. An exploration of these illusions and their devastating impact on the individual is presented. Clinical details are offered, including analysis for strategies for change and how children of alcoholics can discover new choices that allow them to grow beyond the illusions created by parents.

10. Beattie, Melodie. *Codependent No More: How to Stop Controlling Others and Start Caring for Yourself.* New York: Harper Hazelden, 1987.
    This book explores the issue of codependency. A comprehensive checklist, as well as explanations of dysfunctional behaviors and how to overcome them are offered.

11. Beattie, Melodie. *Codependents' Guide to the Twelve Steps.* Englewood Cliffs: Prentice-Hall Press, 1990.
    This work is specifically designed for codependent people. The author offers strategies for helping codependents work through their thoughts and behaviors with the healing process of the 12 steps.

12. Brady, Tom. *Sobriety Is a Learning Process.* Deerfield Beach, FL: Health Communications, Inc., 1985.
    A systematic program for learning to live a sober lifestyle is offered. The work is designed to be used by individuals and groups in the process of recovery.

13. Brown, Stephane, Susan Beletsis, and Timmen Cermak. *Adult Children of Alcoholics in Treatment.* Deerfield Beach, FL: Health Communications, Inc., 1989.
    Working together at the Stanford Alcohol Clinic, these authors attempt to develop useful findings on the treatment of alcoholism. They argue that a more sophisticated approach needs to be taken in the development of knowledge related to alcoholism.

14. Carnes, Patrick. *A Gentle Path through the Twelve Steps: A Guidebook for All People in the Process of Recovery*. Minneapolis, MN: CompCare Publishers, 1989.

  This work discusses how the 12 steps produce the change and growth critical to recovery. Over 40 directive exercises, inventories, and guided reflections are presented.

15. C., Cecil. *Wisdom to Recover*. Minneapolis, MN: CompCare Publishers, 1990.

  The author explores the most talked about topics in recovery today, including anger, denial, and spiritual living. This work is designed for recovering individuals and groups, families, and friends.

16. Cermak, Timmen L. *A Primer on Adult Children of Alcoholics*. Deerfield Beach, FL: Health Communications, Inc., 1989.

  This work covers all aspects of being an adult child from an alcoholic family. The author defines the disease of alcoholism, the five signs of codependence that exist in the family of the alcoholics, and the characteristics that occur in the adult children who grow up in this family. The stages of recovery are analyzed, and solutions are offered to all adult children.

17. Chandler, Mitzi. *Whiskey's Song: An Explicit Story of Surviving in an Alcoholic Home*. Deerfield Beach, FL: Health Communications, Inc., 1987.

  The author writes of her experiences living in an alcoholic home. The focus of the work is on the emotional turmoil that alcoholism creates in the family.

18. Choices. *Choices*. Los Angeles: University of Southern California, 1987.

  The focus of this book is to help kids not to be hustled into drug abuse. The work offers eight lesson models in both Spanish and English.

19. Cohen, Sidney. *The Chemical Brain: The Neurochemistry to Addictive Disorders*. Minneapolis, MN: CompCare Publishers, 1988.

  This work contains a summary of scientific knowledge in neurochemistry and addiction. The focus of the book is an exploration of the biochemical basis of addictions.

20. Conrad, Barnaby. *Time Is All We Have*. New York: Dell, 1986.

  This work explores the author's treatment for alcoholism at the Betty Ford Center. The author attempts to focus on the human side of alcoholism.

21. Dean, Orville A. *Facing Chemical Dependency in the Classroom.* Deerfield Beach, FL: Health Communications, Inc., 1989.

   This work discusses the dilemma of chemical dependency that affects not only the classroom but also the entire society. Included are a Student Assistance Program and suggested curricula. The work attempts to provide help to teachers, administrators, counselors, and parents.

22. Dorris, Michael. *The Broken Cord.* New York: HarperCollins Publishers, Inc., 1989.

   This work reports on what it is like to parent a child with Fetal Alcohol Syndrome. An adoptive parent named Dorris tells her personal story about what it is like to raise a Fetal Alcohol Syndrome child.

23. Ellis, Dan C. *Growing Up Stoned: Coming to Terms with Teenage Drug Abuse in America.* Deerfield Beach, FL: Health Communications, Inc., 1986.

   This work tries to sort out the typical problems of a developing young person from the complications of drug abuse. Practical advice is offered by the author.

24. Ellis, Dan. *Legacies of an Alcoholic Family: A Recovery Novel.* Deerfield Beach, FL: Health Communications, Inc., 1988.

   This work spans from the Prohibition era to the present day, and includes three generations of denial and addiction. The author attempts to analyze the human side of recovery.

25. F., Dan. *Sober but Stuck.* Minneapolis, MN: CompCare, 1991.

   This is a book that identifies 20 major obstacles to growth in recovery, from fear of intimacy and closeness to fear of people and social situations. Each obstacle is illustrated with one or two compelling personal stories of long-time Alcoholics Anonymous members. Each story attempts to provide wisdom, insight, and practical information for recovering people.

26. F., Ed. *God Grant Me the Laughter: A Treasury of Twelve Step Humor.* Minneapolis, MN: CompCare, 1989.

   This is a book for the recovering alcoholic that includes a collection of cartoons, quotes, and asides that tries to capture the relief and joy of recovery, as well as the fellowship potentially offered through the 12–step programs.

27. Fassel, Diane. *Working Ourselves to Death.* San Francisco, CA: Harper San Francisco, 1992.

   This is an exploration of work addicts. The author explains how to distinguish between overwork and work addiction, and provides examples and case histories. Self-tests and charts attempt to guide the reader toward balance and serenity through various techniques, including inventories and daily work plans.

28. Finnegan, John, and Daphne Gray. *Recovery from Addiction*. Berkeley, CA: Celestial Arts Publishing, 1990.

    This work overviews nutritional therapies for recovering and codependency. The authors conclude that any intervention therapy should include a nutritional element. Examples of appropriate nutritional therapies are offered.

29. Ford, Betty. *Betty: A Glad Awakening*. New York: Jove, 1988.

    Betty Ford, the former First Lady, shares her battle with chemical dependency. The author attempts to provide a human side of alcoholism; also emphasized is the importance of helping others.

30. Gold, Mark S. *The Good News about Drugs and Alcohol: Curing, Treating, and Preventing Substance Abuse in the New Age of Biopsychiatry*. New York: Random, 1991.

    Biopsychiatry is applying the rigorous standards of science and medicine to the practice of psychiatry. The author attempts to illustrate how this approach can be used to fight alcohol and drug abuse. The work also covers prevention and education efforts that appear successful in combating chemical abuse in schools, the home, and work place.

31. Gordon, Barbara. *I'm Dancing As Fast As I Can*. New York: HarperCollins Publishers, Inc., 1989.

    A successful career as an award-winning television producer and a good relationship with a man she loved did not stop the author's world from falling apart when she was advised to go off Valium. This work focuses on that experience.

32. Hamel, Richard A. *A Good First Step*. Minneapolis, MN: CompCare Publishers, 1977.

    This is a workbook and guide that is designed to help chemically dependent people understand the key concepts of powerlessness. The work leads the chemically dependent individual through a process away from denial and toward acceptance.

33. Hart, Stan. *Rehab: A Comprehensive Guide to the Best Drug-Alcohol Treatment Centers in the U.S.* New York: HarperCollins Publishers, Inc., 1988.

    This is an analysis of drug-alcohol treatment centers in the United States, aimed at both professionals and laypersons concerned with the problem of alcohol and chemical dependency.

34. Hewett, Paul. *Straight Talk about Drugs*. Minneapolis, MN: CompCare Publishers, 1990.

>   This is a book that offers facts about drugs. The work is particularly designed for parents to give to young people.

35. Jampolsky, Lee. *Healing the Addictive Mind*. Berkeley, CA: Cestial Arts, 1991.

>   This work offers approaches for freeing one's self from addictive patterns and relationships. The author suggests that the human conditions that affect most people, fixed in habits of thinking that keep one stuck, can be changed. The author offers strategies for bringing about these changes.

36. Johnson, Vernon E. *I'll Quit Tomorrow: A Practical Guide to Alcoholism Treatment*. New York: HarperCollins Publishers, Inc., 1990.

>   Written by the founder of the Johnson Institute in Minneapolis, the work presents the concepts and methods that are designed to bring about new hope for alcoholics. The book is for active, potential, or recovering alcoholics.

37. Johnson, Vernon E. *Everything You Need to Know about Chemical Dependence: Vernon Johnson's Complete Guide for Families*. Minneapolis, MN: CompCare Publishers, 1992.

>   This is a work that focuses on the prevention, intervention, and recovery methods for treating chemical dependency. It attempts to teach families about what they need to know before, during, and after chemical dependency.

38. Kasi, Charlotte Davis. *Women, Sex and Addiction: A Search for Love and Power*. New York: HarperCollins Publishers, Inc., 1990.

>   Sexual addiction and codependency are the focus of this work. The book provides a cultural analysis of the problem and offers solutions.

39. Kasi, Charlotte Davis. *Many Roads: One Journey*. New York: HarperCollins Publishers, Inc., 1992.

>   The author takes a look at how 12–step programs work in individual lives, and how they can draw on the steps' wisdom while adapting them to their own experiences, beliefs, and strengths.

40. Kirsch, M. M. *Designer Drugs*. Minneapolis, MN: CompCare Publishers, 1986.

>   An underground chemists, narcotics officers, users, and dealers give no-holds-barred interviews on the newest, deadliest menace on the drug scene.

41. Kominars, Sheppard B. *Accepting Ourselves: The 12-Step Journal of Recovery from Addiction for Gays and Lesbians*. San Francisco, CA: Harper San Francisco, 1989.

    This work attempts to address the needs of substance abuse among the homosexual community. Examined are the unique problems of homosexuals who are confronted with chemical dependency. Approaches for facing their addiction are offered, including the position that one must first accept his or her sexual identity.

42. Kritsberg, Wayne. *Adult Children of Alcoholics Syndrome from Discovery to Recovery*. Deerfield Beach, FL: Health Communications, Inc., 1986.

    The experience of familial alcoholism is described. The solutions for beginning a personal recovery process are outlined in the book.

43. Kritsberg, Wayne. *Gifts: For Personal Growth and Recovery*. Deerfield Beach, FL: Health Communications, Inc., 1988.

    Visualizations, affirmations, journal writing, and other techniques are offered as gifts for those who wish to recover from alcoholism. The work also stresses problems and issues related to codependency.

44. Larranaga, Robert. *Calling It a Day*. San Francisco, CA: Harper San Francisco, 1990.

    The principles of the 12–step program of recovery are used as the basis of this work. The work draws on meditation and spirituality as basic principles to help readers change their ingrained work habits and restore balance to their lives.

45. Lerner, Rokelle. *Daily Affirmation for Adult Children of Alcoholics*. Deerfield Beach, FL: Health Communications, Inc., 1990.

    Affirmations, according to the author, are positive statements that are aimed at changing the way we think. This book of affirmations is designed to be used in one's daily recovery program.

46. Lewis, David C., and Carol N. Williams. *Providing Care for Children of Alcoholics*. Deerfield Beach, FL: Health Communications, Inc., 1986.

    This work tries to fill an important gap in the knowledge base about alcoholism and the family. It provides strategies for reaching out to an often unserved or poorly served group.

47. Marlin, Emily. *Hope: New Choices and Recovery Strategies for Adult Children of Alcoholics*. New York: HarperCollins Publishers, Inc., 1988.

    The author draws on her experiences as a marriage and family counselor, and her own years of being raised by an alcoholic parent. The work overviews the lives and feelings of adult children of alcoholics, and covers the full range of recovery strategies.

48. Marlin, Emily. *Relations in Recovery: New Rules, New Roles for Couples and Families.* New York: HarperCollins Publishers, Inc., 1990.

    This work attempts to show that it is possible to reestablish and restructure relationships that have floundered or failed under the burden of alcohol or other addictions. The significant changes in attitude and behavior that both codependents and the alcoholic or addict must make in order to break negative patterns are covered. The author emphasizes that the alcoholic or addict must heal old wounds, air resentments, and learn to deal with new ones as they arise.

49. May, Gerald G. *The Awakened Heart: Living beyond Addiction.* San Francisco, CA: Harper San Francisco, 1991.

    Love is viewed as an important component of one's social well-being. This book argues that the quest for efficiency and achievement distracts from people achieving love. The author concludes that opening one's heart and trusting others will free one from addictive and compulsive behaviors.

50. Meagher, M. David. *Beginning of a Miracle: How to Intervene with the Alcoholic or Addicted Person.* Deerfield Beach, FL: Health Communications, Inc., 1987.

    Questions are answered by the author focusing on what can be done to stop the alcoholic or addicted individual from a downward spiral. A step-by-step instruction guide is offered.

51. Mellody, Pia, and Andrea Wells Miller. *Breaking Free: A Recovery Workbook for Facing Codependence.* San Francisco, CA: Harper San Francisco, 1989.

    A recovery tool designed to help codependents overcome the sense of devastation they face when first aware of the disease. The work attempts to move individuals beyond denial, to recognize symptoms of the disease in themselves, and move them toward recovery.

52. Mellody, Pia, Andrea Wells Miller, and Keith Miller. *Facing Codependence: What It Is, Where It Comes from, How It Sabotages Our Lives.* San Francisco, CA: Harper San Francisco, 1989.

    The authors explore the origins of codependence, back to patterns learned in childhood. This is designed to be used with their other work, *Breaking Free.* Through their work, the authors have a major goal of helping one understand the nature of codependence.

53. Middelton-Moz, Jane, and Lorie Dwinell. *After the Tears: Reclaiming the Personal Losses of Childhood*. Deerfield Beach, FL: Health Communications, Inc., 1986.

    The focus of this book is on the grief and loss that reflect the family legacy of alcoholism. Children from these systems suffer long-term depression and erosion of their sense of self-worth, according to the author.

54. Milam, James, and Katherine Ketcham. *Under the Influence: A Guide to Myths and Realities of Alcoholism*. New York: Bantam, 1984.

    This book is based on scientific research that examines the physical factors that set alcoholics and nonalcoholics apart. It offers a stigma-free way of understanding and treating alcoholism.

55. Moe, Jerry, and Don Pohlman. *Kids' Power Healing Games for Children of Alcoholics*. Deerfield Beach, FL: Health Communications, Inc., 1989.

    Games and activities are presented specifically for the children of alcoholics and drug-addicted parents. The authors claim that their games have been tested with children ranging from ages 6–12. The games are designed to be noncompetitive, and they stress cooperation. Trust and team work are emphasized, with all players being winners.

56. O'Gorman, Patricia, and Philip Oliver-Diaz. *Breaking the Cycle of Addiction: A Parent's Guide to Raising Healthy Kids*. Deerfield Beach, FL: Health Communications, Inc., 1990.

    This guide attempts to teach parents about breaking the cycle of addiction from generation to generation. The work is aimed at adults who have been affected by an alcoholic or an addicted parent.

57. Parker, Charles E. *Deep Recovery*. Virginia Beach, VA: Hawkeye Press, 1991.

    This book offers new ways for understanding recovery. The word codependency is not used. Dependency is divided into two categories: (1) Lone Ranger and (2) Willing Victim. This approach to understanding dependency offers a different view.

58. Peluso, Emanuel, and Lucy Silvay Peluso. *Women and Drugs: Getting Hooked, Getting Clean*. Minneapolis, MN: CompCare Publishers, 1990.

    This is a book with the aim of helping women addicted to drugs to break through denial, recognize their addiction, and stop its progression. The work is designed for treatment centers, women's groups, and 12–step groups.

59. Pursch, Joseph A. *Dear Doc*. Minneapolis, MN: CompCare Publishers, 1985.

>   This work explores when normal use ends and alcohol and drug abuse begin. The author attempts to offer facts on the complex diseases of alcohol and drug addiction.

60. Schaef, Anne Wilson. *Co-Dependence: Misunderstood-Mistreated*. New York: HarperCollins Publishers, 1986.

>   This work defines codependency as another form of "the addictive process" that is reinforced by the larger society. It discusses the effects of this theory on the fields of chemical dependency, family therapy, mental health, and the women's movement.

61. Schaef, Anne Wilson. *Escape from Intimacy*. San Francisco, CA: Harper San Francisco, 1990.

>   The author explores the problem of relationship addiction and attempts to dissect the cultural supports for this system through a 12–step program for recovery.

62. Schaef, Anne Wilson, and Diane Fassel. *The Addictive Organization*. San Francisco, CA: Harper San Francisco, 1990.

>   The work focuses on the dysfunctional addictive systems in business and other organizations, specifically, how they operate, how to recognize them, and how to begin the recovery process within them.

63. Schutt, Marie. *Wives of Alcoholics: From Co-dependency to Recovery*. Deerfield Beach, FL: Health Communications, Inc., 1986.

>   According to this work, the wives of alcoholics spend most of their time careening from one crisis to another in reaction to their husbands' alcoholism. The hallmarks of the families of these men and women are unmet needs, failure to prosper, and stress. Advice for women is offered for wives after the turmoil of living with an alcoholic spouse.

64. Seixas, Judith S., and Geraldine Youcha. *Children of Alcoholism: A Survivor's Manual*. New York: HarperCollins Publishers, Inc., 1986.

>   Drawing on interviews with hundreds of adult survivors, the authors attempt to address the destructive patterns that can continue through a lifetime. They look at the shame and secrecy that typify the emotional make–up of a child of alcoholism, and discuss such feelings as guilt, embarrassment, and lack of self-esteem.

65. Sheperd, Scott. *Survival Handbook for the Newly Recovering*. Minneapolis, MN: CompCare Publishers, 1988.

>   This book attempts to lead the newly recovering through the perils of the desert of low self-esteem, the swamp of boredom, the bitter wind of loneliness, and the mountains of depression.

66. Sikorsky, Ignor. *AA's Godparent: Three Early Influences on Alcoholics Anonymous*. Minneapolis, MN: CompCare Publishers, 1990.

This work explores the influence of three nonalcoholics, psychiatrist Carl Jung, theologian Emmet Fox, and writer Jack Alexander, on Alcoholics Anonymous. It is designed for people who wish to know more about Alcoholics Anonymous.

67. Smith, Ann. *Grandchildren of Alcoholics: Another Generation of Co-dependency*. Deerfield Beach, FL: Health Communications, Inc., 1988.

This book pinpoints the problems of those living in families where the grandparent is an alcoholic or was an alcoholic. This book defines and attempts to solve the issues.

68. Smith, Carol Cox. *Recovery at Work: A Clean and Sober Career Guide*. San Francisco, CA: Harper San Francisco, 1990.

This is a guide for working toward recovering, rebuilding, and revitalizing one's life. It includes checklists, testimonials, successful stories, self-tests, and guidelines that offer a path to recovery and achieving full career possibilities.

69. Tessina, Tina. *The Real Thirteenth Step: Discovering Confidence, Self-Reliance, and Autonomy beyond the 12-Step Program*. Los Angeles, CA: Jeremy P. Tarcher, Inc., 1991.

Most self-help recovery groups claim that members can never leave the group: if they do, they relapse back to self-destructive habits. The author claims one can graduate from the self-help recovery group and ultimately achieve independence. Skills for learning self-reliance and independence are offered.

70. Thomsen, Robert. *Bill W*. New York: HarperCollins Publishers, Inc., 1985.

This work focuses on the genesis of Alcoholics Anonymous. Insight is offered into the mind of the founder of AA.

71. Vroom, George. *Are You Missing the Boat to Recovery? How to Successfully Take Charge of Your Life*. Deerfield Beach, FL: Health Communications, Inc., 1988.

This work covers the need to take charge during the recovery period. The author deals with the problems of misdiagnosing alcoholism and the adult children of alcoholics syndrome.

72. Washton, Arnold, and Donna Boundy. *Willpower's Not Enough*. New York: HarperCollins Publishers, Inc., 1990.

This is a step-by-step formula for gamblers and workaholics in dealing with their addictions. The book attempts to explain why addiction has become a major social and health problem. Approaches are offered for treating addiction as well as relapse.

73. Weinberg, Jon R., and Daryl Kosloske. *Fourth Step Guide: Journey into Growth*. Minneapolis, MN: CompCare Publishers, 1977.

    This is a workbook that recognizes that recovery is an ongoing process involving changing behavior. Provided are instructions for changing behaviors that contribute to addiction.

74. Welsh, Kathleen W. *Healing a Broken Heart: 12 Steps for Recovery for Adult Children*. Deerfield Beach, FL: Health Communications, Inc., 1988.

    This 12-step book is to be used by Adult Children of Alcoholics support groups in the recovery process. The work emphasizes the Alcoholics Anonymous 12–step approach.

75. Whitfield, Charles L. *Alcoholism, Attachment and Spirituality: A Transpersonal Approach*. Englewood Cliffs, NJ: Thomas W. Perrin, 1985.

    This work offers an in-depth view of the addictive process at work. A connection between chemical dependency and people's need for attachment to the way things should be is offered. The author offers strategies for achieving health, wholeness, and spirituality.

76. Whitfield, Charles L. *Healing the Child Within: Discovery and Recovery for Adult Children of Dysfunctional Families*. Deerfield Beach, FL: Health Communications, Inc., 1987.

    The aim of this work is for those who are in the process of recovery from a troubled or dysfunctional family. The work explores the different forms of abuse, shame, lack of boundaries, codependence, and compulsion. The author offers approaches to recognize the symptoms of codependency and how to heal them.

77. Whitfield, Charles L. A. *Gift to Myself: A Personal Guide to Healing My Child Within*. Deerfield Beach, FL: Health Communications, Inc., 1990.

    This work attempts to provide deeper exploration into how to heal our child within. The goal of the work is to help one experience the gift of creating personal freedom in recovery and in one's life.

78. Woititz, Janet G. *Adult Children of Alcoholics*. Deerfield Beach, FL: Health Communications, Inc., 1990.

    What children of alcoholics need is basic information to sort out the effects of alcoholism. The author attempts to provide this information.

4

Coping with Change

Throughout the life cycle, human beings are confronted with many changes. These changes encompass biological growth, psychological development, and sociocultural experiences. Most changes are very predictable. These include those that occur during the life cycle, for example, a child moving from infancy to early childhood or the family moving from the middle years to the retirement years. Even though such stages of individual and family development are predictable, they still involve stress that must be recognized and dealt with. The less predictable aspects of change deal with unexpected crisis, such as serious illness or unemployment.

Lefrancois (1990, pp. 22–23) outlines some of the predictable, oftentimes temporary, aspects of development and change:

1. Change is continuous, and does not stop with adulthood but continues throughout the entire life span.

2. Causes of development are a result of an individual's interaction with his or her environment and genetic factors.

3. Development occurs in a specific historical and ecological context, and is greatly affected by that context.

4. Common threads appear to run through the developmental paths individuals take. These appear in predictable stages and allow basic generalizations to be made about what individuals experience during these stages.

5. Even though the stages of life are predictable, there are pronounced differences in how individuals experience these stages.

6. Change is the core of human development. Many changes are age and experience related.

Environmental factors play a major role in how well one is capable of coping with change. Those who have physical or mental disabilities, live in poverty, experience illness, and have inadequate training and education have more difficulty coping with change than those not confronted with these problems. It should also be noted that achieving optimum development throughout the life cycle is not only dependent on personal traits; failure to cope with life change may be grounded in prejudicial attitudes of people in one's environment who control opportunities for growth and self-expression (Pardeck, 1992).

Obstacles in the environment may also prevent families from moving through the family life cycle at an optimum level. For example, income loss or poverty has a tremendous impact on the family system. These kinds of factors negatively impact family development. If a family under pressure does not receive the needed economic supports, the family may well break down. Therapeutic supports are also helpful to enable families to survive pressures from the social environment.

Brill (1978, pp. 123–124) offers a useful orientation for helping individuals cope with change. She suggests that practitioners can be assisted through the following when working with clients experiencing change:

1. It is overwhelmingly obvious that one-dimensional intervention strategies are ineffectual when working with problems that are many-dimensional.

2. Individuals cannot be separated from the social context in which they function, and yet the uniqueness of each person cannot be ignored.

3. Clinicians must help clients improve their communication and interactional skills.

4. Clients must take responsibility for their lives in a society that is increasingly more controlling. Self-help is a critical part of effective intervention with clients.

5. Changing a client's social environment can be an effective way for helping clients cope with change.

6. Helping people to change and to cope with change is an important dimension of clinical intervention.

As one can see, the above points are aligned with the use of self-help books. As noted by Brill, treatment should be many-dimensional: self-help books offer another dimension to intervention. Brill also stresses the importance of clients taking control of their lives and the use of self-help in treatment, strategies that clearly endorse the use of books in treatment.

The various works included in this chapter deal with the problem areas experienced by most throughout the life cycle. These areas include loss, life passages, dealing with stress, and other crises associated with the life cycle. Like other self-help titles, these might be used as readings for individuals to understand better the passages of life. Practitioners will also find them useful for conducting individual and group intervention.

REFERENCES

Brill, N. (1978). *Working with people* (2nd ed.). New York: J. B. Lippincott Company.
Lefrancois, G. R. (1990). *The lifespan* (3rd ed.) Belmont, CA: Wadsworth.
Pardeck, J. T. (1992). Using bibliotherapy in treatment with children in residential care. *Residential Treatment for Children and Youth*, 9, 73–90.

BOOKS FOR COPING WITH CHANGE

79. Arsdale, Diana Cort-Van, and Phyllis Newman. *Transitions: A Woman's Guide to a Successful Retirement.* New York: HarperCollins Publishers, Inc., 1991.

    This is a guidebook for women as they approach retirement. The author offers a series of questions to help the reader identify her needs and concerns, and includes case studies.

80. Biracree, Tom, and Nance Biracree. *Over Fifty: The Resource Book for the Better Half of Your Life.* New York: HarperCollins Publishers, Inc., 1991.

    This is a guide providing information and advice on finances, health care, recreation, housing, and social life. Resources and directories are also offered on government agencies and private agencies for older Americans.

81. Bozarth, Alla Renee. *Life Is Goodbye, Life Is Hello: Grieving Well through All Kinds of Loss.* Minneapolis, MN: CompCare Publishers, 1986.

    The author teaches skills in how to grieve well. The guide offers how one can deal with the many kinds of loss, including physical death, death of a relationship, parting, and geographic change.

82. Burns, Maureen A., and Cara M. Burns. *Cara's Story: Coping with Life, Death, and Loss.* New York: HarperCollins Publishers, Inc., 1987.

    The author was a happy, active third grader when a friend and classmate died suddenly from a fall. This is the story of how the child came to terms with death, helped by her family, teachers, and friends. It is a book for all ages.

83. Butler, Robert N. *Why Survive? Being Old in America.* New York: HarperCollins Publishers, Inc., 1985.

> The book discusses the aging process in America. It is designed for readers at various age levels, including high school students and even students attending professional schools.

84. Feinstein, David, and Peg Elliott Mayo. *Rituals for Living and Dying: How We Can Turn Loss and the Fear of Death into an Affirmation of Life.* New York: HarperCollins Publishers, Inc., 1990.

> This work presents the intimate journey of a family contending with the imminent death of a father. The book covers the way ritual can enrich a patient's passage and give his or her family a means of coming to terms with loss.

85. Gates, Philomene. *Suddenly Alone: A Woman's Guide to Widowhood.* New York: HarperCollins Publishers, Inc., 1990.

> This is a guide that covers every aspect of widowhood, including the emotional, social, legal, and financial.

86. Grodin, Charles. *How I Get Through Life: A Wise and Witty Guide.* New York: William Morrow & Company, Inc., 1992.

> This work offers advice for surviving life. Numerous problem areas of life are offered, including ways to meet these problem areas effectively. The work suggests that being happy and treating others well is critical to coping with change.

87. Harris, Diane K. *Sociology of Aging.* New York: HarperCollins Publishers, Inc., 1990.

> The work presents aging in a sociological framework. The work examines new and original facets of the topic, and contains cross-cultural material on the subject of aging.

88. James, John W., and Frank Cherry. *The Grief Recovery Handbook: A Clearly Defined Program for Moving beyond Loss.* New York: HarperCollins Publishers, Inc., 1989.

> The founders of the Grief Recovery Institute present a five-step program for those experiencing the confusion, isolation, and loneliness caused by emotional loss that includes loss of a child, spouse, parent, sibling, job, or other life tie.

89. Larson, Dorothy. *A Touch of Sage: Reflection on Growth, Change, and Growing Older.* New York: HarperCollins Publishers, Inc., 1989.

> The work focuses on life in the later years. The author offers information on confidence, attitudes, reaching out, courage, loss, goal-setting, and enthusiasm.

90. Lightner, Candy, and Nancy Hathaway. *Giving Sorrow Words: How to Cope with Grief and Get on with Your Life*. Minneapolis, MN: CompCare Publishers, 1990.

   This work describes ways individuals cope with grief and loss, The topics covered include the cycle of grief, good grief and bad grief, sudden death, anticipated death, and coping with grief.

91. Mason, L. John. *Guide to Stress Reduction*. Berkeley, CA: Celestial Arts, 1986.

   A series of techniques are offered to reduce stress. Chapters focus on visualization, meditation, biofeedback, autogenics, desensitization, and progressive relaxation.

92. Mason, L. John. *Stress Passages: Surviving Life's Transitions Gracefully*. Berkeley, CA: Celestial Arts, 1988.

   The work concludes that as we pass through life's stages, each carries its own kind of stress. The author explores the many kinds of stress individuals experience and shows different ways to cope with them, from adolescence to marriage to parenting to death.

93. Outerbridge, David E., and Alan R. Hersh. *Easing the Passage*. New York: HarperCollins Publishers, Inc., 1991.

   Designed for the terminally ill and their families, this book provides information on medical and legal steps. The work includes instructions for "The Living Will."

94. Shelley, Florence D. *When Your Parents Grow Old*. New York: HarperCollins Publishers, Inc., 1988.

   This work provides information and resources on issues related to aging, for the elderly as well as their children. The author provides information on public and private support services, financial, legal, and medical matters, and housing alternatives.

95. Siegel, Alan B. *Dreams That Can Change Your Life: A Guide to Navigating Life's Passages through Turning Points and Dreams*. Los Angeles, CA: Jeremy P. Tarcher, Inc., 1991.

   Stories of people who have navigated life's frequent transitions are offered. These include marriage, moving, changing jobs, pregnancy, changing careers, midlife crises, divorce, illness, and loss. Dreams are offered as a vehicle to help individuals deal with change.

96. Tagliaferre, Lewis, and Gary Harbaugh. *Recovering from Loss: A Personalized Guide to the Grieving Process*. Deerfield Beach, FL: Health Communications, Inc., 1990.

   The work offers how different personalities deal with grief, and helps one identify when to let go and seek help. Also offered are strategies for taking charge and how to begin reconstructing one's life.

97. Tatelbaum, Judy. *The Courage to Grieve: Creative Living, Recovery, and Growth through Grief.* New York: HarperCollins Publishers, Inc., 1984.
    The subject of grief is covered in this work. The author offers approaches for understanding and recovering from the profound emotional response that is part of the grieving process.

98. Tatelbaum, Judy. *You Don't Have to Suffer: A Handbook for Moving beyond Life's Crises.* New York: HarperCollins Publishers, Inc., 1990.
    The book suggests that it is possible to live a full and creative life regardless of one's particular circumstances. The work is a guide to achieving such a goal.

99. Zunin, Leonard M., and Hilary Zunin. *The Art of Condolence: What to Write, What to Say, What to Do at a Time of Loss.* New York: HarperCollins Publishers, Inc., 1991.
    This is a guide for helping those who have experienced loss. The goal of the work is to provide strategies for dealing with the process of loss.

5

Family Violence and Dysfunctional Families

A great deal of theory is emerging that is critical of explaining problems related to individual social functioning through an individual pathology approach (i.e., Minuchin, 1974). Newer theories for understanding and explaining problems related to individual social functioning are heavily grounded in the ecological perspective (Howze-Browne, 1988). To understand fully problems related to social functioning, one must look at the individual, familial, social, and cultural factors that all play a part in the creation of problems that confront people in their daily lives.

Research generally suggests that family dysfunction plays a major role in contributing to problems related to the troubled individual. Minuchin offers a detailed model that helps one understand the relationship between individual and familial social functioning. The stress and strain that contribute to dysfunctional families flow from four main sources (Minuchin, 1974). These sources can originate outside and inside the family system. If families are functioning well, individuals within these systems will also generally function well (Pardeck, 1988).

The first source of stress flows from extrafamilial forces on one family member. When one family member is under stress, that member's interactions and transactions with other family members may result in problems that permeate the entire family system. An example of such a situation might be the husband under stress at work who criticizes his wife when he gets home; she in turns criticizes him, and the result of this transaction is a fight. The disagreement can be resolved by positive closure and mutual supports, or it might generate more family stress that influences the entire family system negatively. Obviously the resources of each family member will greatly determine the interaction and transactions with the individual family member who is under pressure.

The second source of stress, according to Minuchin, is extrafamilial forces on the whole family system. Family systems are at times simply overloaded by external pressures that affect the entire family. An example of this would be economic depression generated through unemployment of the breadwinner of a family. Stress from external forces may also be caused by the family's moving to

a new neighborhood or when the poverty-stricken family is confronted by numerous social services agencies, resulting in an overload of the family's coping
mechanisms.

Minuchin suggests that stress at transitional points in the family is a third
source of pressure on virtually all family systems. In a certain sense, this kind of
stress is predictable and is related to the evolution of the family system. These
stages of family growth are as follows:

1. Establishment (childless, newly married)

2. First parenthood (infant to three years of age)

3. Family with preschool child (child's age three to six years)

4. Family with school-aged child (child's age 6–12 years)

5. Family with adolescent (child's age 13–20 years)

6. Family as launching center (children leave home)

7. Family in middle years (empty nest)

8. Family in retirement (breadwinner 65 and older)

The transition through each of these stages is far from stress free; if anything,
stress and conflict are inevitable. How well the family handles each stage of the
family life cycle has great implications on how well individuals adjust to their
social environment.

A good example of stress created by the family's evolution through the life
cycle is when a child moves into adolescence. If parents and child are not able to
accommodate and adapt to the adolescence period, the family may experience
stress and strain. If the family system reacts to the adolescent experience in a
healthy fashion, most of the pressure related to adolescence can be dealt with effectively.

The final source of family stress is related to idiosyncratic problems.
Dysfunctional family patterns may appear around idiosyncratic issues unique to
a given family system, such as a family with a disabled child. When the child is
young, the family may be able to adapt to the disabled child with little problem.
However, when the child begins interacting with social systems outside the family, the child may not be able to adapt; hence, this stress on the child may overload the family system.

In summary, families are subject to pressures both external and internal to
the family system. The family's ability to adapt and change will greatly determine how stress is managed by the family system. If families do not adjust well
to these pressures, the likely outcome is family dysfunction. Problems related to
the dysfunctional family include wife battering, child abuse, and chemical abuse.

Numerous self-help books are available on a variety of issues related to dysfunctional families. Chapter 3 provides excellent titles for helping families confront chemical dependency. Many of the annotated self-help books in this chapter focus on problems related to family violence. The majority of these books focus on helping adult victims who were abused as children, whereas a limited number focus on battered women.

We know that treating children who have been abused is a very difficult task. Many of these children do not trust themselves or people in their social environment. Abused children often view their environment as inconsistent and feel those around them wish to harm them. They find it is safer to withdraw from the world than to be a part of it. Germain, Brassard, and Hart (1985) conclude that abused children often have emotional symptoms that include anger, denial, repression, fear, self-blame, self-doubts, helplessness, low self-esteem, guilt, dejection, and apathy. If these problems are not resolved during childhood, they will follow the individual into adulthood. For many individuals, child abuse does indeed create long-term psychological and behavioral problems that must be dealt with through therapeutic intervention (Pardeck, 1988).

Domestic violence is also an emerging social problem. *Battering* is the current term used to describe domestic violence. Battering includes but is not limited to the practice of slapping, punching, knocking down, choking, kicking, hitting with objects, threatening with weapons, stabbing, and shooting (Walker, 1979). What has emerged out of the literature focusing on domestic violence is the term *battered woman syndrome*, which is defined as the systematic and repeated use of one or more of the above against a women by her husband or lover. It is estimated that millions of women are battered each year (Walker, 1979).

Women who are likely to be battered often seem to have certain characteristics (Walker, 1979). Low self-esteem is common among this group. Their husbands tend to criticize them and make derogatory remarks, behaviors that obviously reinforce their low self-esteem. Martin (1976, p. 81) found that battered women often feel they are responsible for the abuse and feel it is their responsibility to maintain the marriage. Another common characteristic of these women is that they tend to believe men should take the lead in the family, and that women should be submissive and obedient.

The abusive husband also has a tendency to have certain traits (Walker, 1979). These men appear to have low self-esteem, identify with the common myths about battering, and to have rigid traditional gender-role stereotypes. They are often emotionally immature and tend to use the act of battering as a means of alleviating stress. Abusive men are often insecure and frequently are very jealous of their wives. Gelles (1976) concludes that many of these men have learned to use aggression as a coping mechanism from their families of orientation.

Battered women have numerous problems that need to be resolved. They often feel guilt, lack self-confidence, fear the abuser, fear for their children, and fear the isolation and economic problems that may result if they leave their husbands. They often are overwhelmed and confused, and need support in dealing with the conflict that they are attempting to resolve. Often the problems that confront them must be dealt with one at a time, and decisions related to their marriage must be made step by step. One of the most important issues that battered women must realize is that they do have choices and that they do not have to live with a male who batters them. The books presented in this chapter can help battered women in treatment resolve the psychological problems related to family violence. Many of these titles can also help practitioners and people in general better understand the problem of family violence, including adults who were abused as children.

REFERENCES

Gelles, R. (1976). Abused wives: Why do they stay? *Journal of Marriage and the Family*, 38, 659–658.

Germain, R., M. Brassard, and S. Hart (1985). Crisis intervention for maltreated children. *School Psychology Review*, 14, 291–299.

Howze-Browne, D. (1988). Factors predictive of child maltreatment. *Early Child Development and Care*, 31, 43–54.

Martin, D. (1976). *Battered wives*. San Francisco, CA: Glide Publications.

Minuchin, S. (1974). *Families and family therapy*. Boston, MA: Harvard University Press.

Pardeck, J. T. (1988). An ecological approach for social work practice. *Journal of Sociology and Social Welfare*, XV(2), 133–142.

Walker, L. (1979). *The battered women*. New York: Harper & Row.

BOOKS ON FAMILY VIOLENCE AND DYSFUNCTIONAL FAMILIES

100. Ackerman, Robert. *Same House Different Homes*. Deerfield Beach, FL: Health Communications, Inc., 1987.

      This work is based on a study of over one thousand adults who are children of alcoholics. Based on this study, the author presents positive solutions for adult children of alcoholics who grew up in dysfunctional homes.

101. Adams, Kenneth M. *Silently Seduced: When Parents Make Their Children Partners: Understanding Covert Incest*. Deerfield Beach, FL: Health Communications, Inc., 1991.

      The focus of this work is on the serious social problem of incest. The work provides incest victims with information on how their lives continue to be affected and how to begin the process of recovery.

102. Adults Anonymous Molested As Children. *Adults Anonymous Molested As Children: The Twelve Step Program for Healing and Recovery.* Minneapolis, MN: CompCare, 1991.

    This text is designed to treat adults who were victimized as children. Based on the 12–Step program, strategies for healing are offered. First-person accounts of members who have been victims of sexual abuse, questions and answers, and guidance are presented for establishing mutual help groups.

103. Amber. *Please Say You're Sorry.* Minneapolis, MN: CompCare, 1992.

    This work is designed for women who have survived incest. Through handwritten and self-illustrated testimony, the author provides her own story concerning victimization.

104. Baker, Sally A. *Family Violence and the Chemical Connection.* Deerfield Beach, FL: Health Communications, Inc., 1992.

    The author illustrates the relationship between chemical abuse and family violence. The work claims that family violence is a common problem, and strategies are presented for dealing with the problems associated with family violence.

105. Bass, Ellen, and Laura Davis. *The Courage to Heal: A Guide for Women of Child Sexual Abuse.* New York: HarperCollins Publishers, Inc., 1988.

    The goal of this book is to empower survivors of child sexual abuse. Various strategies are presented to help survivors deal with the aftermath of this serious social problem.

106. Bass, Ellen, and Louise Thorton. (eds.). *I Never Told Anyone: Writings by Women Survivors of Child Abuse.* New York: HarperCollins Publishers, Inc., 1991.

    This work offers testimonies of child sexual abuse. A list of resource groups and treatment centers for treating child abuse is offered.

107. Bradshaw, John. *Bradshaw on the Family: A Revolutionary Way of Self-Discovery.* Deerfield Beach, FL: Health Communications, Inc. 1988.

    Based on the television series of the same name, the author attempts to illustrate the dynamics of how family attitudes learned while growing up become encoded within each family member. According to the author, the unhealthy rules that can contribute to various family dysfunctions, including abuse, are handed down from one generation to the next. Strategies are offered for changing these dysfunctional behaviors.

108. Braheny, Mary, and Diane Halperin. *Mind, Body, Spirit: Connecting with Your Creative Self.* Deerfield Beach, FL: Health Communications, Inc., 1989.

    This is a self-help tool for adult children who have grown up in dysfunctional families. The guide provides experiential exercises for each developmental stage using movement, body releases, art, visualization, and affirmations.

109. Davis, Laura. *The Courage to Heal Workbook: For Women and Men Survivors of Child Sexual Abuse.* New York: HarperCollins Publishers, Inc., 1990.

    This book is designed to help those who were victims of child abuse. It offers a combination of checklists, writing exercises, art projects, and activities that offer a step-by-step guide to the healing process.

110. Davis, Laura. *Allies in Healing: When the Person You Love Was Sexually Abused As a Child.* New York: HarperCollins Publishers, Inc., 1991.

    This work addresses the needs of partners and spouses of survivors of child sexual abuse. Various strategies are offered to deal with this serious social problem.

111. Friel, John, and Linda Friel. *Adult Children: The Secrets of Dysfunctional Families.* Deerfield Beach, FL: Health Communications, Inc., 1988.

    The text defines the problems of dysfunctional families. Combining theory and clinical practice, this book attempts to offer an explanation for why some families are dysfunctional.

112. Graber, Ken. *Ghosts in the Bedroom: A Guide for Partners of Incest Survivors.* Deerfield Beach, FL: Health Communications, Inc., 1991.

    This work is designed to present a step-by-step guide to comfort and guide partners of incest survivors. Various insights and activities are presented to accomplish this goal.

113. Hunter, Mic. *Abused Boys: The Neglected Victims of Sexual Abuse.* Minneapolis: MN: CompCare Publishers, 1989.

    Each year thousands of boys are sexually abused. Often, later in life, these children have difficulty achieving intimacy with their partners. The author attempts to offer help and healing for adults recovering from child maltreatment. A number of first-person stories are presented, and an extensive resource guide is also offered.

114. LairRobinson, Barbara and Rick LairRobinson. *If My Dad's a Sexaholic, What Does That Make Me?* Minneapolis, MN: CompCare, 1989.

    This book offers an outline of the specific problems and characteristics of adult children of sex addicts. The goal is to offer hope to these adults who have been victims of this serious problem. Clinical information and case studies with firsthand experiences and personal stories are offered. The characteristics of adult children who have been victimized and a recovery model are presented.

115. Lasater, Lane. *In Sickness and in Health: The Co-dependent Marriage.* Deerfield Beach, FL: Health Communications, Inc., 1988.

After comparing the relationships that work with those that do not, this book, through examples, gives practical guidelines to building relationships. A major focus of the author is on the marital relationship.

116. Lew, Mike. *Victims No Longer: Men Recovering From Incest And Other Sexual Child Abuse.* Minneapolis, MN: CompCare Publishers, 1990.

The author suggests that our culture has no room for male victims of child abuse. Often male victims are expected to deal with the problem of incest on their own, that is, to deal with it like a man. The work seeks to dismiss this myth, and to help male victims deal with the denial, grief, loss, anger, and other issues that result from sexual abuse.

117. Maltz, Wendy. *The Sexual Healing Journey: A Guide for Survivors of Sexual Abuse.* New York: HarperCollins, 1991.

This is a how-to, personal therapy book that offers a number of cases on the problems associated with those who have survived sexual abuse. The author stresses that abuse may become buried in a victim's unconscious self and thus contribute to sexual dysfunction. The work attempts to offer what constitutes sexual abuse and the myths that surround this serious social problem.

118. Mellody, Pia, Andrea Miller, and Keith Miller. *Facing Co-dependence.* San Francisco, CA: Harper San Francisco, 1989.

The book offers an analysis of and explanation for why certain family systems are dysfunctional. The major thrust of the authors is on the issue of codependence, tracing the origins of the illness back to childhood, and describing a whole range of emotional, spiritual, intellectual, physical, and sexual abuses.

119. Middelton-Moz, Jane. *Children of Trauma: Rediscovering Your Discarded Self.* Deerfield Beach, FL: Health Communications, Inc., 1988.

The work focuses on childhood trauma, including abuse. The author attempts to explain how unresolved trauma in childhood can reverberate throughout one's life and the lives of one's children without anyone being aware of its origins.

120. Middelton-Moz, Jane. *Shame and Guilt: Master of Disguise.* Deerfield Beach, FL: Health Communications, Inc., 1989.

This book describes how debilitating shame and guilt are created and fostered in childhood. The author offers practical advice for dealing with these psychological issues.

121. Miller, Joy, and Marianne Ripper. *Following the Yellow Brick Road: The Adult Child's Personal Journey through Oz*. Deerfield Beach, FL: Health Communications, Inc., 1987.

> The authors attempt to provide a guide to recovery. The guide is based on the characters in *The Wizard of Oz*.

122. Mones, Paul A. *When a Child Kills: Abused Children Who Kill Their Parents*. New York: Pocket Books, 1991.

> The plight of children caught in the web of child maltreatment is explored. Cases of abused children who kill their parents are presented. The goal of the work is to offer new insights into this important social problem.

123. Nestingen, Signe, and Laurel Lewis. *Growing beyond Abuse*. Minneapolis, MN: CompCare Publishers, 1991.

> This is a workbook for survivors of sexual exploitation and childhood sexual abuse. The work offers poetry and prose, healing reading, and written exercises to help individuals deal with the pain of victimization.

124. NiCarthy, Ginny, and Sue Davidson. *You Can Be Free: An Easy-to-Read Handbook for Abused Women*. Minneapolis, MN: CompCare Publishers, 1989.

> This book presents basic insights into the problems of women who have been victims of abuse. The author attempts to offer support, answers, and actions that women can take when they are being abused by someone they love.

125. O'Gorman, Patricia, and Philip Oliver Diaz. *The 12 Steps to Self-Parenting for Adult Children*. Deerfield Beach, FL: Health Communications, Inc., 1990.

> Designed for those who have had a traumatic childhood, this work uses the 12 steps of gentle healing and self-parenting for recovery. The goal of the authors is to help the adult child move from anger to forgiveness, from fear to faith, and from despair to recovery.

126. Petersen, Betsy. *Dancing with Daddy: A Childhood Lost and A Life Regained*. New York: Bantam, 1991.

> This book is about incest and the effects that it has on the victims of this serious problem. The work is an account of the author's own victimization, and the mental and emotional pain she has suffered as a result of incest.

127. Porterfield, Kay. *Violent Voices: 12 Steps to Freedom from Verbal and Emotional Abuse.* Deerfield Beach, FL: Health Communications, Inc. 1989.

> The focus of this work is on abusive relationships. The dynamics and effects of being in a relationship with a verbally or psychologically abusive partner are openly discussed.

128. Ratner, Ellen. *The Other Side of the Family: A Book for Recovery from Abuse, Incest, and Neglect.* Deerfield Beach, FL: Health Communications, Inc., 1990.

> The issues related to surviving child maltreatment are presented. Offered are treatment strategies for combating the problem of victimization.

129. Roche, Helena. *The Addiction Process from Enabling to Intervention.* Deerfield, FL: Health Communications, Inc., 1989.

> This book looks at all the elements of the addiction process, the addiction, the addicted person, the family, and the therapist. It discusses the emotional and behavioral difficulties that develop as the dependency progresses.

130. Roy, Maria. *Children in the Crossfire: Violence in the Home–How Does It Affect Our Children?* Deerfield Beach, FL: Health Communications, Inc., 1988.

> Alcoholism and family violence affect numerous children each year. This book attempts to help one do something about this serious problem.

131. Russell, Pamela, and Beth Stone. *Do You Have a Secret? How to Get Help For Scary Secrets.* Minneapolis, MN: CompCare, 1986.

> All children are potential victims of abuse; thus, the authors feel they need to know what to do about it. The work is designed to help children tell scary secrets, such as having been a victim of abuse. Included are an adult guide and illustrations concerning abuse.

132. Subby, Robert. *Healing the Family Within.* Deerfield Beach, FL: Health Communications, Inc., 1990.

> The emphasis of the book is on recovery. The author concludes that recovery begins with confronting the dysfunctional patterns of our inner families, and letting go of the toxic shame and guilt that we carry around from our past.

133. Whitfield, Charles L. *Healing the Child Within: Discovery and Recovery for Adult Children of Dysfunctional Families.* Deerfield Beach, FL: Health Communications, Inc., 1987.

> The author argues that within each of us lies our true self, waiting to be fully discovered and appreciated. Often, however, this in-

ner child is buried beneath layers of guilt, resentment, shame, and isolation that began in childhood. A guide is offered for discovering the inner child.

134. Williams, Mary Jane. *Healing Hidden Memories: Recovery for Adult Survivors of Childhood Abuse.* Deerfield Beach, FL: Health Communications, Inc., 1990.
     This work provides approaches for dealing with the pain of abuse. The work is based on personal accounts of the author.

135. Woititz, Janet. *The Self-Sabotage Syndrome: Adult Children in the Workplace.* Deerfield Beach, FL: Health Communications, Inc., 1989.
     The author describes employees who are adult children of alcoholics as often overachievers, very successful, dedicated, loyal to a fault, and able to take on responsibilities that rival Superman—but at what cost? The text suggests that adult children of dysfunctional families are at times people who lack any sense of balance in their personal or professional lives. This book attempts to help these individuals.

136. Woititz, Janet Geringer. *Healing Your Sexual Self.* Deerfield Beach, FL: Health Communications, Inc., 1989.
     The aftermath of sexual abuse has long-term effects and often prevents individuals from entering healthy relationships with others. The author suggests that a clear and direct strategy for dealing with this problem is to recognize that something has gone wrong and to deal it. Survivors of sexual abuse are shown how to recognize the problem and to deal effectively with its many psychological components.

137. Wolter, Dwight Lee. *A Life Worth Waiting For! For All Adult Children of Alcoholics and Other Dysfunctional Families.* Minneapolis, MN: CompCare, 1988.
     This book is written for survivors of dysfunctional families. The book deals with a number of problems, with an emphasis on solving them through reading and written activities.

6

Parenting

Parenting is hard work. The pressures of work, finding appropriate day care, and meeting the needs of children in a changing world make parenting a difficult task. Within the United States, parents are presented with more obstacles than parents in other developed countries. The United States lack comprehensive day care, family leave, income supports, quality health care for all children, and other basic supports that are taken for granted by parents in other industrialized countries. Until comprehensive services are made available to all parents within the United States, the pressures of parenting will not abate (Pardeck, 1990).

Regardless of the current problems associated with parenting within the United States, parents must do the best job possible under harsh social conditions. What are the problem areas associated with parenthood? One clear crisis is the birth of the first child. Many transitions must be made by new parents. One transition is that adulthood becomes official; new parents must not only care for themselves, but also a new child. The arrival of a new baby means 24-hour care. A baby demands a huge amount of care and attention. If both parents work, their schedules must change, while new roles and responsibilities emerge that have never been dealt with before. It must be clearly noted that even in the most liberated families, the bulk of caring for children falls on the mother. Hobbs and Cole (1976) conclude that wives versus husbands have greater difficulty adjusting to parenting because of the added demands resulting from motherhood. Similar findings have been reported by Russell (1974).

It must also be noted that having children is an economic liability. Furthermore, parenting has both a negative and positive impact on one's lifestyle. For these reasons, present-day families are growing smaller. Even though the attitudes toward marriage and lifestyles have changed over the years, many couples still feel compelled by the larger society to have children (Pardeck, 1990).

There are numerous pressures associated with parenting; however, a number of studies have found positive aspects to being a parent. Hoffman and Manis (1979) found that love of children, fun, and stimulation are all positives aspects of parenting. Price-Bonham and Skeen (1979) found that fathers rated as the best part of parenting the feeling of love for their child and that love being returned. They also found that children made fathers feel respected and that children would offer them a great deal as fathers grow older. Discipline problems and increased responsibilities were the negatives of fathering.

Feldman (1971) finds that children greatly impact marriage. Husbands and wives often disagree over the parenting process; this conflict can have a negative impact on marriage. The tension that children bring to a marriage is less if the new parents have known each other for an extended time period. Those new parents who are excessively dependent on each other experience increased marital satisfaction following the birth of a baby. Like Feldman, Rollins and Galligan (1978) conclude that children have a major impact on degree of marital satisfaction. The birth of a child results in less marital satisfaction for working-class parents in particular. If the child is wanted by parents and if support systems are in place, children are less likely to impact parenting negatively. Finally, Feldman (1971) reports that even when parenting has a negative impact on marital satisfaction, parenting still contributes to the personal development of an individual through improving one's self-concept and work roles.

Parenting as a process has been found to develop along four distinct stages (the Group for the Advancement of Psychiatry, 1973). These include:

1. *Anticipation.* This is the first stage, which occurs during pregnancy and involves the parents beginning to think about how they will raise their children. Many expectant parents are nervous about their new role and are uncertain about what parenting will involve. The expectant parents also begin to view themselves as their children's parents, instead of being parents of a new child.

2. *Honeymoon.* The second stage occurs after the birth of the child. It typically lasts for a few months. Parents during this stage are happy to have a new baby and enjoy providing for the child. It is a time of adjustment and learning: bonding begins between parents and child, and parents begin learning new roles.

3. *Plateau.* This stage occurs from infancy through the adolescent years. Both parents and children must adjust to each other during this stage.

4. *Disengagement.* The final stage occurs when the child leaves the home. When the child leaves the home for marriage or for other reasons, parents change their behavior and allow the child to leave the home. Obviously, the parent-child relationship changes to an adult-adult relationship.

The critical aspect concerning the above stages is that children have a great affect on parents. In turn, parents must realize they have a tremendous impact on a child's growth and development; however, there are many factors outside the parenting process that shape the socialization process of children. In essence, parents may do all the correct activities for raising a well-adjusted child, yet factors external to the parenting process may have a positive or negative impact on the child's development.

Clearly, the parenting process is extremely complex and involves numerous factors external to the control of parents. It is also well known that parents within the United States, unlike parents in other industrialized nations, lack many supports critical to successful parenting. Even with the added pressure of parents being victims of an unresponsive society, they must utilize whatever tools are available to help them to improve the parenting process. Self-help books are clearly such a tool. A number of studies have illustrated the power of self-help books as a tool for effectively improving parenting.

Gordon (1970) reports research on the effectiveness of his book *Parent Effectiveness Training (PET)*. In his work, Gordon encourages parents not to nag, lecture, or scold, but instead to use a problem-solving approach when working with their children. Gordon advises parents when to listen with empathy and when to assert their rights as a parent, using "I" statements. Gordon suggests that when children need acceptance, parents should use techniques of active listening, or they may demonstrate acceptance through nonintervention or passive listening. The road blocks to communication include ordering, directing, commanding, warning, threatening, giving solutions, criticizing, ridiculing, and lecturing. He offers strategies for improving communication.

Gordon describes three ways of resolving parent/child conflict with I win-you lose, you win-I lose (both ineffective), and the effective win-win situation in which both the child and parent resolve the conflict together. Finally, Gordon's (1970) program has been found to be a useful tool for consulting with parents; it is also a widely used program.

Dinkmeyer and McKay (1976), in their book *Systematic Training for Effective Parenting (STEP)*, stress an Adlerian model grounded in the work of Rudolf Dreikurs. Their work stresses the principles of logical consequences over punishment and of using cooperation versus power in the child-rearing process. The *STEP* program teaches parents to recognize the goals of misbehavior and how to change these behaviors. Critical components of the *STEP* program include weekly family meetings, daily individual time with parents, and weekly fun activities. Dinkmeyer and McKay (1976), in their work, provide research to support the efficacy of their program.

Finally, many of the annotated books listed in this chapter deal with the critical problems facing children. The books included can serve as useful supports for helping parents raise their children. Many of the titles can also serve as useful adjuncts to working with parents through individual or group approaches to treatment. Many of the titles can be particularly useful as core readings for parenting education classes.

REFERENCES

Dinkmeyer, D., and G. McKay (1976). *Systematic training for effective parenting*. Circle Pines, MN: American Guidance Service.

Feldman, H. (1971). The effects of children on the family. In *Family issues of employed women in Europe and America*, ed. A. Michel, 60-82. Leiden, The Netherlands: E. F. Brill.

Gordon, T. (1970). *Parenting effectiveness training*. New York: Wyden.

Group for the Advancement of Psychiatry. (1973). *The joys and sorrows of parenthood*. New York: Scriber's.

Hobbs, D., and S. Cole (1976). Transitions to parenthood: A decade of replication. *Journal of Marriage and the Family*, 38, 723–731.

Hoffman, L., and J. Manis (1979). The value of children in the United States: A new approach to the study of fertility. *Journal of Marriage and the Family*, 41, 583–596.

Pardeck, J. T. (1990). An analysis of the deep structure preventing the development of a national policy for children and families in the United States. *Early Child Development and Care*, 57, 23–30.

Price-Bonhan, S., and P. Skeen (1979). A comparison of black and white fathers with implications for parent education. *The Family Coordinator*, 28, 53–59.

Rollins, B., and R. Galligan (1978). The developing child and marital satisfaction of parents. In *Child influences on marital and family interaction: A lifespan perspective*, ed. R. Lerner and G. Spanier, 71-105. New York: Academic Press.

Russell, C. (1974). Transition to parenthood: Problems and gratification. *Journal of Marriage and the Family*, 36, 294-302.

BOOKS ON PARENTING

138. Arms, Suzanne. *Adoption: A Handful of Hope*. Berkeley, CA: Celestial Arts, 1989.

> This work contains a series of case studies that offer the personal and moving accounts of children who have been adopted, adoptive parents, and women who have given their babies for adoption. The author attempts to show how the process of adoption can be improved for all parties involved.

139. Armstrong, Thomas. *In Their Own Way: Discovering and Encouraging Your Child's Personal Learning Style*. Los Angeles, CA: Jeremy P. Tarcher, Inc., 1987.

> This work is designed for parents and teachers who are experiencing problems in school. Various learning styles are covered, including Kinetic and Linguistic, that help to inform adults of how children learn. Strategies for helping children acquire knowledge are covered.

140. Armstrong, Thomas. *Awakening Your Child's Natural Genius: Enhancing Your Child's Curiosity, Creativity, and Learning Ability*. Los Angeles, CA: Jeremy P. Tarcher, Inc., 1991.

    This work includes techniques for helping youngsters achieve their full potential. It is created for baby-boomer parents. At-home activities for parents to do with toddlers and children in grades K–6 are offered. Resources are listed to help parents in the parenting process.

141. Baldwin, Rahima. *You Are Your Child's First Teacher*. Berkeley, CA: Celestial Arts, 1989.

    This book stresses that parents are offered numerous approaches on how to parent their children. The author offers a new way of understanding the human being so that parents can be better parents. The work is based on the Montessori theoretical approach.

142. Becnel, Barbara Cottman. *The Co-Dependent Parent: Free Yourself By Freeing Your Child*. San Francisco, CA: Harper San Francisco, 1991.

    The author is a recovering codependent parent. The work attempts to show how to make the transition from good parent, one who requires that children behave in highly defined ways to gain approval, to responsible parent, one who teaches children guidelines for maintaining self-respect and integrity.

143. Berends, Polly Berrien. *Whole Child Whole Parent*. New York: HarperCollins Publishers, Inc., 1987.

    This work offers a holistic guide to child raising. It is designed for parents and others who work with children.

144. Blechman, Elaine A. *Solving Child Behavior Problems at Home and at School*. Champaign, IL: Research Press, 1985.

    This book provides step-by-step methods for improving children's behavior. It includes guidelines to help prevent common behavior problems from escalating into more serious ones.

145. Brondino, Jeanne, Shellie Brann, Scott Coatsworth, Heidi Sonzeno, Cheryl Swain, and Frances Tulao. *Raising Each Other: A Book for Teens and Parents*. Minneapolis, MN: CompCare Publishers, 1990.

    This book is taken directly from real-life exchanges between parents and high school students. In this work, parents and teens share their perspectives on issues of freedom, privacy, trust, responsibility, money, sex, and religion.

146. Canter, Lee, and Marlene Canter. *Assertive Discipline for Parents.* New York: HarperCollins Publishers, Inc., 1988.

This is a guide to enable parents to use new approaches to raising their children. The work offers strategies for helping parents not to be manipulated by their children and to use positive support when children behave.

147. Caron, Ann F. *Don't Stop Loving Me: A Reassuring Guide for Mothers of Adolescent Daughters.* New York: HarperCollins Publishers, Inc., 1992.

The author attempts to explore the issues that affect mothers and daughters, including trust, dependency, sex, peers, friends, competition, chemicals, and discipline. The work illustrates the ups and downs of mothers and their adolescent daughters.

148. Carson, Rachel. *The Sense of Wonder.* New York: HarperCollins Publishers, Inc., 1987.

This is a book that offers the natural wonders around all of us. The work is designed to help adults who have children or work with children.

149. Collins, Marva, and Ciuia Tamarkin. *Marva Collins' Way: Returning to Excellence in Education.* Los Angeles, CA: Jeremy P. Tarcher, Inc., 1990.

The author recounts her successful teaching approaches. Strategies are offered to help motivate all children to reach their full potential. The work is designed for both parents and teachers.

150. Dayton, Tian. *Daily Affirmations for Parents: How to Nurture Your Children and Renew Yourself during the Ups and Downs of Parenthood.* Deerfield Beach, FL: Health Communications, Inc., 1991.

The author attempts to help parents develop positive thoughts and uplifting affirmations. The work is designed to help parents through the ups and downs of parenthood.

151. Dinkmeyer, Don, and Gary P. McKay. *Systematic Training for Effective Parenting.* Circles Pines, MN: American Guidance Service, 1990.

This work stresses an Adlerian model for effective parenting. It offers principles of logical consequences over punishment and of using cooperation versus power in the child-rearing process.

152. Dunn, Judy, and Robert Plomin. *Separate Lives: Why Siblings Are So Different.* New York: Basic Books, 1992.

The authors argue that the home environment plays a bigger role in a child's development versus genes. The work is based on research on the topic of why siblings differ in their development.

153. Glenn, H. Stephen, and Jane Nelsen. *Raising Self-Reliant Children in a Self-Indulgent World*. Rocklin, CA: Prima Publishing, 1989.

   This book goes beyond the leniency versus strictness issue to teach children to be responsible and self-reliant. The author attempts to teach parents how to raise responsible, self-reliant children.

154. Gordon, Thomas. *Parenting Effectiveness Training*. New York: Wyden, 1970.

   This work describes appropriate communication for parents when working with children. Problem-solving approaches are offered for improving the parenting process.

155. Hart, Louise. *The Winning Family: Increasing Self-Esteem in Your Children and Yourself*. Deerfield Beach, FL: Health Communications, 1990.

   This book provides specific, practical methods for developing communication and leadership skills in families. Included are leadership skills as well as other skills for effective living, self-esteem, and mental health.

156. Hausner, Lee. *Children of Paradise: Successful Parenting for Affluent Families*. Los Angeles, CA: Jeremy P. Tarcher, Inc., 1990.

   Affluence may have its rewards; however, it also presents significant child-rearing problems. Analyzed are the unique problems typical of affluent families. Ten principles of effective parenting are offered.

157. Ilg, Frances L., Louise Bates Ames, and Sidney Baker. *Child Behavior: The Classic Childcare Manual from the Gesell Institute of Human Behavior*. New York: HarperCollins Publishers, Inc., 1982.

   This is a book that offers strategies for enhancing the lives of children and improving their behavior. It is designed for parents, teachers, and others who care for children.

158. Kaplan, Paula. J. *Don't Blame Mother*. New York: HarperCollins Publishers, Inc., 1990.

   This work explores the myths that surround the mother-daughter relationship. It offers guidelines for enhancing and deepening the relationship between mothers and daughters.

159. Kurcinka, Mary Sheedy. *Raising Your Spirited Child: A Guide for Parents Whose Child Is More Intense, Sensitive, Perceptive, Persistent, Energetic*. New York: HarperCollins Publishers, Inc., 1991.

   A parenting authority offers approaches for parenting the difficult child. The reader will find skills for minimizing conflict, fostering healthy relationships, and improving the lives of parents and their difficult children.

160. Leonard, Joan. *Tales from Toddler Hell: My Life as a Mom*. New York: Pharos Books, 1991.

> This is an attempt to use humor to help mothers of toddlers deal with this critical stage of the life cycle. The work attempts to reassure mothers that others have faced similar problems when raising toddlers.

161. Mason, Daniel A. *Double Duty: Parenting Our Kids While Reparenting Ourselves*. Minneapolis, MN: CompCare Publishers, 1990.

> This work is for parents recovering from addiction and/or codependency, and for therapists who need practical wisdom for working with recovering parents. The book focuses on the chaotic lifestyles and other typical problems that stand in the way of effective parenting for recovering people.

162. Muse, Nina J. *Depression and Suicide in Children and Adolescents*. Austin, TX: Pro-Ed, 1990.

> Mental health professionals have recently recognized that depression is not the exclusive domain of adults, but also affects children. This handbook is for parents and professionals who come into routine contact with youth. The work covers symptoms that may indicate the presence of depression and the specter of suicide.

163. Patterson, Gerald R. *Families: Applications of Social Learning to Family Life*. Champaign, IL: Research Press, 1975.

> This work contains social learning procedures designed to help bring about desired changes in the family unit. The author uses a program learning format that helps parents to recognize the crucial role they play in shaping their children's behavior.

164. Patterson, Gerald R. *Living with Children: New Methods for Parents and Teachers*. Champaign, IL: Research Press, 1976.

> This manual shows how children learn behavior and how they actually train parents to behave. It is written for parents and teachers who have little or no background in social learning theory.

165. Pogue, Carolyn. *The Weekend Parent: Learning to Live without Full-time Kids*. Minneapolis, MN: CompCare Publishers, 1992.

> This is a guide to helping noncustodial parents play a more meaningful role in the lives of their children. The book presents 20 stories of men and women who have lost custody of their children.

166. Rattray, Jamie, Bill Howells, and Irv Siegler. *Kids and Alcohol*. Deerfield Beach, FL: Health Communications, Inc., 1983.

> This book is designed to promote health and well-being through active, responsible choice, instead of allowing oneself to becoming a victim. The book, for elementary and junior high school aged

readers, attempts to help children become more accountable and responsible for their behavior.

167. Rattray, Jamie, Bill Howells, and Irv Siegler. *Kids and Drugs*. Deerfield Beach, FL: Health Communications, Inc., 1983.

With the theme being get high on life, this book attempts to illustrate how young readers can feel good about themselves, and become choosers and not victims. It attempts to help parents help children to have confidence to say no to drugs.

168. Reaves, John, and James Austin. *How to Find Help for a Troubled Kid*. New York: HarperCollins Publishers, Inc., 1991.

This book is designed for parents dealing with their troubled adolescents. The work covers topics such as teenage pregnancy, depression, mental illness, drug and alcohol abuse, and school problems. The index provides information on counseling hotlines, treatment centers, and drug and alcohol programs.

169. Rolfe, Randy. *Adult Children Raising Children: Sparing Your Child from Co-dependency without Being Perfect Yourself*. Deerfield Beach, FL: Health Communications, Inc., 1989.

This book attempts to help parents who were raised with alcoholism or other behavioral dysfunction prevent the same kind of problems from affecting their own children. Strategies are offered for dealing with daily family situations that purport to impact children positively.

170. Sanger, Sirgay, and John Kelly. *The Woman Who Works, the Parent Who Cares*. New York: HarperCollins Publishers, Inc., 1992.

A psychiatrist offers a program that attempts to demonstrate how the lifestyle of today's working woman can actually encourage the development of a more self-confident, independent, and socially developed child.

171. Schaefer, Charles E. *How to Talk to Children about Really Important Things*. New York: HarperCollins Publishers, Inc., 1992.

This work is designed to foster better communication between parents and their five- to ten-year-old children. The topics covered include going to the hospital, moving, alcoholic parent, death, abuse, divorce, prejudice, religion, and war.

172. Schwebel, Andrew; Bernice Schwebel, Carol Schwebel, Milton Schwebel, and Robert Schwebel. *A Guide to a Happier Family: Overcoming the Anger, Frustration, and Boredom That Destroy Family Life*. Los Angeles, CA: Jeremy P. Tarcher, Inc., 1986.
    Their work with families is explored by the authors. The issues covered include separation and divorce, communication, intimacy, and related issues.

173. Scott, Lucy, and Meredith Joan Angwin. *Time Out for Motherhood*. Los Angeles, CA: Jeremy P. Tarcher, Inc., 1986.
    Advice on pregnancy issues is offered. These include medical concerns for average-aged and older mothers-to-be. Techniques are offered for handling emotions related to pregnancy.

174. Sifford, Darrell. *The Only Child: Being One, Loving One . . . Understanding One, Raising One*. New York: HarperCollins Publishers, Inc., 1990.
    Only children are different and have unique needs. The book draws on case studies, interviews with psychologists, and other helping professions. The work is designed to help parents of only children.

175. Simpson, Richard L., and Paul Zionst. *Autism: Information and Resources for Parents, Families, and Professionals*. Austin, TX: Pro-Ed, 1992.
    Parents, families, and professionals are provided information on autism. The book is in a question-and-answer format. The authors respond to questions about autism asked by countless parents and family members of children and youth with autism. The authors summarize what is known and report the progress being made to understand and deal with autism better.

176. Sloane, Howard N. *The Good Kid Book: How to Solve the 16 Most Common Behavior Problems*. Champaign, IL: Research Press, 1988.
    This is a manual for parents who need help with specific child behavior problems. Each chapter is a self-contained behavior guide with step-by-step procedures for helping children overcome specific behavioral problems.

177. Smith, Judith M., and Donald E. P. Smith. *Child Management: A Program for Parents and Teachers*. Champaign, IL: Research Press, 1976.
    This work attempts to show how to help children learn appropriate behavior. The manual contains a programmed format. Values and moral training are offered. Examples of problem situations that teach children to consider consequences in making decisions are presented.

178. Steinberg, Laurence, and Ann Levine. *You and Your Adolescent: A Parent's Guide for Ages 10–19*. New York: HarperCollins Publishers, Inc., 1990.
    This is a manual for parents raising adolescents. The work attempts to explore most of the major developmental crises confronting both parents and their adolescent children.

179. Toma, David, and Christopher Biffle. *Turning Your Life Around*. New York: HarperCollins Publishers, Inc., 1992.
    This book attempts to offer approaches to help children stop self-destructive behaviors that affect their development and social functioning. Facts about drug and alcohol abuse are offered, including case studies of adolescents who were able to overcome self-destructive behaviors and approach life with new hope and optimism.

180. Toth, Michele. *Understanding and Treating Conduct Disorders*. Austin, TX: Pro-Ed, 1990.
    Conduct disorder youth are a challenge for parents and professionals. This booklet answers the following questions: What is a conduct disorder and how does it develop? What are the signs of a conduct disorder? The work is designed to identify and break the cycle of misbehavior that leads to labels of incorrigibility.

181. Weinhaus, Evonne, and Karen Friedman. *Stop Struggling with Your Child*. New York: HarperCollins Publishers, Inc., 1991.
    The authors recommend strategies for reducing parent/child and child/child conflict. These are based on the authors' experiences in working with clients. Vignettes are offered that illustrate how one can improve the social functioning of children.

182. Wheelan, Susan A., and Melvin L. Silberman. *How to Discipline without Feeling Guilty: Assertive Relationships with Children*. Champaign, IL: Research Press, 1980.
    This is a guide for helping parents and teachers evaluate their relationships with children. It highlights the similarities and differences between parenting and teaching, while it addresses the specific needs of both. Examples illustrate the techniques for disciplining children.

183. Williams, Mary L. *My Precious Child: Affirmations for the Child Within*. Deerfield Beach, FL: Health Communications, Inc., 1991.
    This is a book for children and adults about nurturing. Various affirmations are offered to facilitate growth and development.

184. Young, Roger. *From Curiosity to Confidence: Help to Build Self-Esteem through Early Reading by Using Home Computers*. Berkeley, CA: Celestial Arts Publishing, 1992.
    This book shows how to make learning fun through the use of computer games and educational software. The work suggests that most

of the latest software for kids is exciting, interactive, and affordable–and much can be done without parental supervision. The work is aimed at building a child's self-esteem through computer technology.

185. Youngs, Bettie B. *Helping Your Teenager Deal with Stress.* Los Angeles, CA: Jeremy P. Tarcher, Inc., 1989.
    Teenagers are often troubled by stress. This work attempts to guide parents through various approaches designed to help parents with children experiencing stress.

186. Zarrow, Teryl. *The Mother Side of Midnight.* Reading, MA: Addison-Wesley, 1992.
    The struggles and rewards of parenting are offered. Familiar parenting activities are covered; these include mealtime, family activities, birthday parties, and caring for pets. The author attempts to offer parenting situations with which the reader can identify.

187. Zionst, Paul, and Richard L. Simpson. *Understanding Children and Youth with Emotional and Behavioral Problems: A Handbook for Parents and Professionals.* Austin, TX: Pro-Ed, 1990.
    This work is designed for parents, families, and professionals. The goal of the book is to further one's understanding of troubled children and the services available to meet their needs. The work is designed to provide straightforward, basic information about childhood and adolescent emotional and behavioral problems.

7

Personal Growth

The process of personal growth is a lifelong goal for most individuals. Personal growth involves improving communication skills, improving assertion and personal relationship skills, learning to improve leadership skills, and improving positive thinking about oneself and others. Even though personal growth is largely aimed at healthy people, learning to continue to adjust and cope with problems can be a related goal to personal growth. These problems might include parental divorce, eating disorders, and other related problems that can be a barrier to personal growth.

Within the field of psychology, the concept that is aligned with personal growth is *self-actualization*. Personal growth, like self-actualization, means the fullest, most complete differentiation and harmonious blending of all aspects of one's total personality. Personal growth means the psyche has evolved to a new center; that is, the self takes the place of the old center, the ego. The person who has achieved optimal personal growth is similar to Jung's (1954) view of what human beings might evolve to once the process of self-actualization is complete. That essentially is a person who has fulfilled one's fullest potentials and is accepting of the self.

Abraham Maslow (1971) provides another view of what personal growth is about. He believes it is human nature for people to seek to know the self better and to strive to develop one's fullest potential. Maslow concludes that human nature is essentially good, and that the striving for self-actualization is a positive process that leads to people identifying their fullest potentials, feeling good about the self, and contributing positively to the larger society. These are all goals for one wishing to achieve personal growth.

Maslow (1971) views most individuals as being in a constant state of striving to improve one's self. However, few people achieve the personal growth needed to become self-actualized. The majority of people are in a constant state of disequilibrium and are striving to resolve this state through personal growth.

Maslow's hierarchy of needs provides additional insight into the goals of personal growth and what it means to achieve one's fullest potential. His hierarchy of needs involves five levels at which one might find the self. The hierarchy of needs are as follows:

1. *Physiological*: water, food, oxygen, and rest.

2. *Safety*: security, stability, and freedom from fear, threats, chaos, and anxiety.

3. *Belongingness and love*: intimacy and affection provided by friends, lover, and family.

4. *Self-esteem*: respect of others, achievement, self-respect, and appreciation.

5. *Self-actualization*: the sense that one is fulfilling one's potential and is doing what one is individually suited for.

A self-actualized person displays high levels of all of the following characteristics: accepts self and others; seeks justice, order, truth, unity, and beauty; has abilities to solve problems; has a richness of emotional responses; has satisfying relationships with other people; and has a high sense of moral values.

Each lower need must be satisfied before moving to the next need level. Consequently, physiological needs must be satisfied before one can move to safety needs. Maslow's state of self-actualization is not age-related but can occur at nearly all ages. However, obviously there are some limitations when one considers the developmental life cycle. For example, infants have a strong emphasis on physiological needs, and are not capable of achieving more advanced needs that involve advanced levels of cognitive and emotional development, whereas adults can achieve higher–level needs because they have moved to the advanced stages of the life cycle. Unfortunately, personal growth leading to self-actualization may be interrupted by personal crises, such as broken relationships, unemployment, and illness. Maslow (1971) concludes that one might regress to lower levels of the hierarchy through individual crises.

Maslow believes that most psychologists study the stunted, crippled, and neurotic individuals, which ultimately results in a crippled psychology. Thus, personal growth and self-actualization have not received the emphasis needed to have a complete field of psychology. Maslow thus focuses on healthy people rather than sick ones; consequently, these two groups generate two types of theories—one aimed at growth and development, and the other focused on pathology.

Maslow (1971), however, concludes that persons who achieve personal growth leading to self-actualization are rare. Examples of characteristics that distinguish them from others are as follows:

1. They have a realistic orientation.

2. They accept self and others.

3. Spontaneity is a part of their lives.

4. They are problem-centered, not self-centered.

5. A need for privacy and an air of detachment is part of their lifestyle.

6. They are independent and autonomous.

7. They appreciate people and abhor stereotypes of others.

8. Most have had a religious or mystical experience.

9. They identify with humankind.

10. Their intimate relationships with a few specially loved people tend to be profound and deeply emotional.

11. Their attitudes and values are democratic.

12. They do not confuse means with ends.

13. Having a sense of humor is a part of their lifestyle.

14. They are creative.

15. They resist conformity.

Obviously, individuals possessing the above characteristics are rare. Few achieve all of these characteristics. However, those who are attempting to realize their full potential through personal growth are attempting to achieve the above distinguishing characteristics.

Presently, numerous self-help books offer strategies for achieving personal growth and development. The titles included in this chapter offer strategies to help one become more accepting of the self and others, move toward a problem-centered approach to life rather than a self-centered approach, and to increase one's creativity and resist conformity to the larger culture.

Some of the titles in this chapter also deal with personal growth issues that may be indicative of more clinical problems, such as codependency, and recovery from abuse and dependency. These kinds of titles are offered because they focus on issues that one might have learned to cope with, but may be striving to go beyond simple coping to a level of personal growth and development that might lead to self-actualization. Thus, these kinds of titles are offered to the emotionally able person who has had negative experiences that block personal growth. The titles included in this chapter might be self-administered, or used in personal growth groups, self-help groups, and other kinds of groups aimed at achieving one's highest level of personal, emotional, and social development.

REFERENCES

Jung, C. (1954). *Collected works: Psychology and alchemy.* New York: Pantheon Press.
Maslow, A. (1971). *The farther reaches of human nature.* New York: Viking.

BOOKS ON PERSONAL GROWTH

188. Andre, Rae. *Positive Solitude: A Practical Psychology for Avoiding the Six Traps of Loneliness and Achieving Self-fulfillment.* New York: HarperCollins Publishers, Inc., 1992.

     The author attempts to offer a practical guide to show how one should cope with the problem of loneliness. The author provides approaches for replacing desperation with inspiration to turn solitude into a positive force that provides self-fulfillment and increased self-esteem.

189. Ball, Carolyn M. *Claiming Your Self-Esteem: A Guide Out of Codependency, Addiction, and Other Useless Habits.* Berkeley, CA: Celestial Arts, 1991.

     This is a guide to improving self-esteem. The work attempts to help individuals learn to respect the self, replace failure with success, create fulfilling relationships, and experience inner peace.

190. Basch, Michael Franz. *Understanding Psychotherapy: The Science behind the Act.* New York: Basic Books, 1990.

     The author, a psychiatrist, attempts to show how and why psychotherapy works. The book is written for those who are currently undergoing, or considering, treatment.

191. Baudhuin, John. *Romantic Relationships in Recovery: The Thirteenth Step.* Minneapolis: MN: CompCare Publishers, 1991.

     This book informs and advances the recovery process. The author examines how relationship patterns are reflected in one's life.

192. Beaumont, J. Graham. *Brainpower: Unlocking the Secrets of the Mind.* New York: HarperCollins Publishers, Inc., 1990.

     This book explains how the brain works, from the basic functions of language, memory, motor skills, and reasoning to extraordinary feats of photographic memory and super IQ. Concepts such as daydreaming, deja vu, and aging are also explored.

193. Becker, Robert A. *Addicted to Misery: The Other Side of Co-dependency.* Deerfield, FL: Health Communications, Inc., 1989.

     The author tries to isolate what addiction to misery is, and to help one see and understand how to stop the misery. According to the work, this process will set one free from hurt and pain that seems to never end. Tools are offered that are supposed to prevent one from returning to unhappiness and misery.

194. Biffle, Christopher. *A Journey through Your Childhood: A Write-in Guide for Reliving Your Past, Clarifying Your Present, and Charting Your Future*. Los Angeles, CA: Jeremy P. Tarcher, Inc., 1989.

This is a book for recovering memories of childhood in order to gain a deeper, vividly detailed sense of personal history. Steps are provided to help the reader to explore personal nostalgia that details that special time he or she may feel is gone forever.

195. Bly, Robert. *Iron John. A Book about Men*. Reading, MA: Addison-Wesley, 1990.

By retelling the Grimm Brothers' tale, the author explores the pain and confusion among contemporary men and points the way toward discovering a long tradition of male ways of feeling.

196. Bolles, Richard Nelson. *The 1992 What Color Is Your Parachute?* Berkeley, CA: Ten Speed Press, 1992.

This work is designed to help people change their lives. The book in particular is written for job-hunters and those who wish to change careers.

197. Bono, Edward de. *Lateral Thinking: Creativity Step-by-Step*. New York: HarperCollins Publishers, Inc., 1973.

This work introduces ways of reasoning and decision making; the author concludes that generating idea after idea "laterally" is a creative alternative to "vertical" or purely logical thinking in which the goal is to arrive at one correct solution to a given problem.

198. Booth, Leo. *When God Becomes a Drug: Breaking the Chains of Religious Addiction and Abuse*. Los Angeles, CA: Jeremy P. Tarcher, Inc., 1991.

The author describes addiction to religion. Religion under these conditions is used to escape from reality and to raise one's self-worth. The work suggests the outcome of this kind of addiction as a refusal to doubt or question authority, judgmental attitudes, and using fear, shame, and guilt as a means to control others. Religious addiction, according to the author, is comparable to alcohol addiction.

199. Bowden, Julie, and Herbert Gravitz. *Genesis: Spirituality in Recovery from Childhood Traumas*. Deerfield Beach, FL: Health Communications, Inc., 1988.

The book deals with the last phase of recovery whereby one discovers and recovers one's relationship with one's Higher Power. The authors claim that the emotions of peace and joy develop as a person's awareness, and lifestyles change toward a more loving and caring existence.

200. Bradshaw, John. *Homecoming: Reclaiming and Championing Your Inner Child*. New York: Bantam, 1992.

> The inner child is the focus of the work. Offered are the core of the author's workshops on the inner child. The goal of the work is to enhance spiritual growth, personal freedom and adult functioning.

201. Brandon, Nathaniel. *The Power of Self-Esteem: An Inspiring Look at Our Most Important Psychological Resource*. Deerfield Beach, FL: Health Communications, Inc., 1992.

> The author claims most everyone comes from dysfunctional families; however, it is still possible to develop positive self-esteem. Self-esteem is defined, including where it comes from and how we get it. Strategies are offered for improving self-esteem.

202. Bryan, Nancy. *Thin Is a State Mind*. Minneapolis, MN: CompCare Publishers, 1992.

> Most overweight people are caught in an anxiety-producing double-bind, according to the author. This includes dieting in a spirit of self-pity or bingeing in a spirit of self-hate. The work claims it is possible to give up the stress of trying to control one's weight through will power and, instead, allow one's body to take charge of weight loss by listening to "inner signals."

203. Bryant, Roberta Jean. *Stop Improving Yourself and Start Living*. New York: New World Library, 1991.

> This is a self-improvement book. The author presents in narrative form her story of recovery, relapse, and change. Self-improvement focuses on the emotional, mental, and spiritual aspects of social functioning and improvement.

204. Butler, Pamela E. *Talking to Yourself: Learning the Language of Self-Affirmation*. San Francisco, CA: Harper San Francisco, 1991.

> This is a guide that attempts to help individuals shed light on the self-defeating images of the past. The author covers how one can change one's life by learning to reprogram the internal, self-defeating tapes, or dialogues, that one carries around with one from childhood.

205. Carson, Richard D. *Taming Your Gremlin: A Guide to Enjoying Yourself*. New York: HarperCollins Publishers, Inc., 1986.

> According to the author, the gremlin within one wants one to feel bad. Through this powerful metaphor, the author tries to help the reader find ways to identify and banish the self-defeating aspects of one's personality.

206. Castine, Jacqueline. *Recovery from Rescuing.* Deerfield Beach, FL: Health Communications, Inc., 1989.

> This book is for those who are tired of the burden of caring for others. The author offers strategy for taking control, when to let go, and how to break the cycle of guilt and fear that keeps one in the responsibility trap.

207. Catford, Lorna, and Michael Ray. *The Path of the Everyday Hero: Drawing on the Power of Myth for Solving Life's Most Important Challenges.* Los Angeles, CA: Jeremy P. Tarcher, Inc., 1991.

> This is a guide that attempts to answer five major challenges of life. Each of the challenges is compared to great myths. These myths include the Holy Grail, Beauty and the Beast, the Peasant Who Married a Goddess, the Story of Theseus, and Cinderella. Understanding each of these myths is purported to help one understand one's true purpose, how to find love, keys to living in the present, balancing personal and professional life, and the meaning of prosperity.

208. Chandler, Mitzi. *Gentle Reminders For Co-dependents: Daily Affirmations.* Deerfield Beach, FL: Health Communications, Inc., 1989.

> The focus of this work is on codependence. The author, through personal insight, attempts to take the codependent child through the year with a daily affirmation and a message of hope.

209. Chernin, Kim. *Reinventing Eve: Modern Woman in Search of Herself.* New York: Harper Collins Publishers, Inc., 1988.

> This is a self-discovery guide that explores the meaning of women's hunger (both literal and figurative).

210. Cherry, Kittredge. *Hide and Speak.* San Francisco, CA: Harper San Francisco, 1991.

> This book covers the problems associated with keeping or telling secrets upon ourselves and others. A major focus of the work concerns the problems facing lesbians and gays who wish to "come out." Advice is offered to lesbians and gays about this process. Self-discovery exercises are included.

211. Chin, Richard. *The Energy Within: The Science behind Every Oriental Therapy from Acupuncture to Yoga.* New York: Paragon House, 1992.

> This book explains the basics of Oriental treatment. Oriental treatment is founded upon knowledge of one's body energy system, including the mental and spiritual components. Exercises are offered, as well as recommendations for diet.

212. Chopich, Erika J., and Margaret Paul. *Healing Your Aloneness: Finding Love and Wholeness through Your Inner Self*. San Francisco, CA: Harper San Francisco, 1990.

    This book describes how the adult often becomes estranged from the inner child. Outlined is a self-healing process that can be used every day to restore a nurturing balance between the loving adult and loved inner child.

213. Covington, Stephanie. *Awakening Your Sexuality: A Guide for Recovering Women*. San Francisco, CA: Harper San Francisco, 1992.

    This book is for women who wish to explore the issue of sexuality. Using case studies, the author tries to guide the reader through childhood and family sexual issues, body image and awareness, sexual history and behavior patterns, desire, and improving one's sex life.

214. Cruse, Joseph. *Painful Affairs: Looking for Love through Addiction and Co-dependency*. New York: Double Day, 1989.

    Chemical dependency and codependency are both illnesses, according to this work. The former is a disorder of the brain and it functioning mind; the latter is a disorder of the brain and its functioning personality. The author describes the symptoms, signs, and complications of these two diseases.

215. Csikszentmihalyi, Mihaly. *Flow: The Psychology of Optimal Experience: Steps toward Enhancing the Quality of Life*. New York: HarperCollins Publishers, Inc., 1990.

    The author explores the states of "optimal experience," concentration so focused that it amounts to absolute absorption in an activity. The author offers a set of scientific discoveries about human nature that illuminates the life experiences of all persons.

216. Dayton, Tian. *Drama Games: Techniques for Self-Development*. Deerfield Beach, FL: Health Communications, Inc., 1989.

    Feelings are often attached to roles, according to the author. Thus, when we experiment with different roles, we naturally become more aware of a variety of feelings, both in expressing and experiencing them. This work attempts to help individuals get in touch with and express hidden feelings in a safe and structured way, and to offer ways in which individuals can be creative and spontaneous.

217. Downing, Christine (ed.). *Mirror of the Self: Archetypal Images That Shape Your Life*. Los Angeles, CA: Jeremy P. Tarcher, Inc., 1989.

    Drawing upon the theories of Jung, this collection of papers explores the many images of the inner world, and their creative and destructive aspects. Known in the popular culture as the gods and goddesses within, the full range of archetypes includes symbolic figures, such as the ego, shadow, and inner male and female. The work attempts to help the reader identify these forces within us, learn how to decide which to nurture and change, and discover how to tap his or her power to live a fuller life.

218. Dyer, Wayne W. *Pulling Your Own Strings: Dynamic Techniques for Dealing with Other People and Living Life as You Choose.* New York: HarperCollins Publishers, Inc., 1991.

> The author attempts to offer a direct and practical guide for dealing with other people. The work also offers strategies for living life as one chooses.

219. Dyer, Wayne W. *Your Erroneous Zones: Step by Step Advice for Escaping the Negative Thinking and Taking Control of Your Life.* New York: HarperCollins Publishers, Inc., 1991.

> The author provides step-by-step advice for escaping the trap of negative thinking. Also offered are strategies for taking control of life.

220. Edwards, Betty. *Drawing on the Right Side of the Brain.* Los Angeles, CA: Jeremy P. Tarcher, Inc., 1989.

> This work attempts to explain how one can learn to draw more accurately and creatively. Sample drawings, research on handedness, learning disabilities, and male-female differences are offered.

221. Field, Joanna. *An Experiment in Leisure.* Los Angeles, CA: Jeremy P. Tarcher, Inc., 1983.

> The value of memories of everyday experiences in the development of self-understanding and creativity is explored in this book.

222. Field, Joanna. *On Not Being Able to Paint.* Los Angeles, CA: Jeremy P. Tarcher, Inc., 1983.

> This is an exposition, using painting as a metaphor, of how one can free the creative process. The author focuses on writing, sculpture, dance, and other creative endeavors as a medium for freeing the creative process.

223. Field, Joanna. *A Life of One's Own.* Los Angeles, CA: Jeremy P. Tarcher, Inc., 1991.

> This work offers strategies for helping one to use journal writing as a means of self-discovery. Methods are offered for finding and living by one's true personal values. The work draws from the author's personal journal entries, sketching analyses, and physical and mental exercises.

224. Fields, Rick. *The Code of the Warrior: A Way of Personal Development through Classical Warrior Traditions: Japanese Samurai, Plains Indians, and Medieval Knights*. New York: HarperCollins, 1991.

      The traditional codes of warriors in earlier societies are adapted to modern society. The purpose of the work is to create new paths to spiritual and personal development.

225. Fiore, Neil. *The Now Habit: A Strategic Program for Overcoming Procrastination and Enjoying Guilt-Free Play*. Los Angeles, CA: Jeremy P. Tarcher, Inc., 1989.

      A strategic system is offered for overcoming the causes of and for the elimination of procrastination. The techniques covered are designed to help individuals get things done more quickly without the anxiety and stress brought on by delay and pressing deadlines.

226. Fishel, Ruth. *Learning to Live in the Now: 6-Week Personal Plan to Recovery*. Deerfield Beach, FL: Health Communications, Inc., 1987.

      Exercises are offered to heal the past, and learn to live now and enjoy today without worry for the future or regret for the past. The author stresses that there is only this moment and it should be enjoyed.

227. Fishel, Ruth. *Time for Joy: Daily Affirmations*. Deerfield Beach, FL: Health Communications, Inc., 1990.

      This work contains illustrations that take the reader through a calendar year with quotations and healing, energizing affirmations. These messages address fears and imperfections of being human. The author attempts to help the reader become self-accepting and at peace.

228. Fisher, Stanley, and James Ellison. *Discovering the Power of Self-Hypnosis: A New Approach for Enabling Change and Promoting Healing*. New York: HarperCollins Publishers, Inc., 1992.

      Through a simple 90-second exercise, the author attempts to show how one can do self-hypnosis. Through this process, the author concludes that we can talk to our bodies and minds to alleviate such problems as phobias, insomnia, performance anxiety, depression, stress, overeating, and smoking, as well as medical conditions.

229. Fox, Arnold, and Barry Fox. *Wake Up! An MD's Prescription for Healthier Living through Positive Thinking*. Deerfield Beach, FL: Health Communications, Inc., 1988.

      The authors try to show how one's thoughts can make one healthy by strengthening one's immune system. The authors claim that even those who are confronted with life-threatening diseases can benefit from the book.

230. Freedman, Rita. *Bodylove: Feeling Good about Your Looks and Yourself.* New York: HarperCollins Publishers, Inc., 1990.

> This guide is for women who wish to change their body image and feelings about the self.

231. Freeman, Arthur, and Rose DeWolf. *The 10 Dumbest Mistakes Smart People Make and How to Avoid Them: Using Cognitive Therapy to Gain Greater Control of Your Life.* New York: HarperCollins Publishers, Inc., 1992.

> Cognitive therapeutic techniques are presented. The focus is on the common habits of thinking that cause social maladjustment. These include the Chicken Little syndrome, perfectionism, comparisonism, and what-if thinking. A quiz is offered that directs the reader to the appropriate chapter for solving a problem area. Techniques are recommended for changing one's thinking and behavior.

232. Gergen, Kenneth J. *The Saturated Self: Dilemmas of Identity in Contemporary Life.* New York: Basic Books, 1992.

> This is an analysis of how the realities of postmodern life are changing the way we view ourselves and our relationships. A goal of the work is to attempt to explain the contradictions of modern life.

233. Golabuk, Philip. *The Sunset Grill Chronicles: Some Food for Thought about Love and Relationships.* Tarrytown, NY: Wynwood Press, 1992.

> A definition of love is presented in this work. The definition is grounded in philosophy, psychology, and literature. The focus of the book centers on four middle–age individuals attempting to make sense out of life.

234. Goldberg, Philip. *The Intuitive Edge: Understanding Intuition and Applying It in Everyday Life.* Los Angeles, CA: Jeremy P. Tarcher, Inc., 1989.

> Approaches to decision making and problem solving are offered. The authors claim intuition can provide a crucial edge, enhancing our ability to discover, create, predict, and evaluate complex problems. The author attempts to illustrate how one can recognize and cultivate intuition.

235. Goldstein, Ross, and Diane Landau. *Forty-Something: Claiming the Power and Passion of Your Midlife Years.* Los Angeles, CA: Jeremy P. Tarcher, Inc., 1991.

> The unique possibilities and advantages enjoyed by the 76 million baby boomers as they experience the midlife years are explored. The author offers ten skills for dealing with the midlife years. These include but are not limited to self-image.

236. Gotkin, Janet, and Paul Gotkin. *Too Much Anger, Too Many Tears: A Personal Triumph over Psychiatry.* New York: HarperCollins Publishers, Inc., 1992.

      This work is a written account of a young woman's mental breakdown, years of psychiatric mistreatment, and eventual self-cure. The book is a statement against psychiatry.

237. Grof, Christina, and Stanislav Grof. *The Stormy Search for the Self.* Los Angeles, CA: Jeremy P. Tarcher, Inc., 1992.

      The authors explore transformative states to develop insight into spiritual emergence, and its complications and vicissitudes. This work is written for people whose lives are touched by spiritual emergency. The goal of the book is to serve as a guide for individuals involved in personal transformation of a milder and less dramatic form.

238. Grof, Stanislau, and Christina Grof. *Spiritual Emergency: When Personal Transformation Becomes a Crisis.* Los Angeles, CA: Jeremy P. Tarcher, Inc., 1991.

      Psychologists, psychiatrists, and spiritual teachers explore the relationships among healing, madness, and spirituality. The editors attempt to help the reader experience spiritual emergence and renewal.

239. Hagan, Kay Leigh. *Internal Affairs: A Journalkeeping Workbook for Self-Intimacy.* San Francisco, CA: Harper San Francisco, 1990.

      Techniques are offered for journal keeping. The author attempts to illustrate how one can dig into one's past, and it is suggested that this information will ultimately help one to outline a personal map for the future.

240. Harman, Willis, and Howard Rheingold. *Higher Creativity: Liberating the Unconscious for Breakthrough Insight.* Los Angeles, CA: Jeremy P. Tarcher, Inc., 1984.

      Examined is the most prized but least understood human trait, creativity. The inner works of the creative mind are explored, including a voyage through the brains and minds of creative individuals.

241. Hendlin, Steven J. *The Discriminating Mind: A Guide to Deepening Insight and Clarifying Outlook.* New York: Mandala Books, 1987.

      A clinical psychologist examines the meaning of identity and the nature of self-belief. These issues are explored through case studies and practical exercises to help the reader become familiar with the self.

242. Hyams, Joe. *Zen in the Martial Arts.* Los Angeles, CA: Jeremy P. Tarcher, Inc., 1979.

      This work attempts to illustrate how one can maximize zest and minimize stress. The author explains how one can become enlightened.

243. Ingerman, Sandra. *Soul Retrieval: Mending the Fragmented Self through Shamanic Practice*. San Francisco, CA: Harper San Francisco, 1991.

    The author explores combining soul retrieval with contemporary psychological concepts to enable clients to overcome depression, memory repression, addictions, and other physical and psychological problems.

244. James, Muriel, and John James. *Passion for Life: Psychology and the Human Spirit*. New York: Dutton, 1992.

    This book offers seven basic spiritual urges that the authors feel shape human existence: (1) urge to live, (2) understanding, (3) creativity, (4) enjoyment, (5) connection, (6) transcending, and (7) freedom. The authors show that each of these are manifested in humans and the ways in which one can achieve them.

245. Jampolsky, Gerald. G. *Love Is Letting Go of Fear*. Berkeley, CA: Celestial Arts Publishing, 1989.

    This work attempts to teach how to let go of fear and how to remember that one's very essence is love. Included are daily exercises that give a direct and effective method for bringing about this individual transformation.

246. Jampolsky, Gerald G., and Diana Cirincione. *Me First and the Gimmes*. Deerfield Beach, FL: Health Communications, Inc., 1991.

    Attitudinal healing is the focus of this work. The authors outline seven stepping stones of inner health.

247. Johnson, Robert A. *Transformation: Understanding the Three Levels of Masculine Consciousness*. San Francisco, CA: Harper San Francisco, 1991.

    Using the literary archetypes of Don Quixote, Hamlet, and Faust, the author examines the three distinct levels of human consciousness development that each of these figures represent. The levels of consciousness explored are the simple; the complex or three dimensional; and the redeemed or four dimensional.

248. Kaye, Yvonne. *The Child That Never Was: Grieving Your Past to Grow into the Future*. Deerfield Beach, FL: Health Communications, Inc., 1990.

    The author attempts to provide an in-depth look at the grieving process adult children go through during recovery. The work provides approaches for helping one to let go of the past and enjoy the rest of one's life.

249. Keen, Sam. *Fire in the Belly: On Being a Man*. New York: Bantam, 1991.
This book is written as a guide book to the men's conscious-ness movement. The author looks at the stereotypes, myths, and evolv-ing roles of contemporary men, and presents an alternative vision of virtue and virility for a modern age. New models of masculine spirit are offered, including what is wrong with men and women and their rela-tionships.

250. Klinger, Eric. *Daydreaming: Using Waking Fantasy and Imagery for Self-Knowledge and Creativity*. Los Angeles, CA: Jeremy P. Tarcher, Inc., 1991.
Daydreams are the theme of this book. The author focuses on common concerns related to sexual daydreams, daydreaming to distrac-tion, obsessive daydreams, and daydreams that are frightening or disturb-ing. The benefits of daydreams are offered.

251. Kopp, Sheldon. *Even a Stone Can Be a Teacher: Learning and Growing from the Experience of Everyday Life*. Los Angeles, CA: Jeremy P. Tarcher, Inc., 1985.
Events and activities of daily life experiences can be a source of growth and wisdom. The author attempts to show how almost every-thing, from time spent watching soap operas to our reactions to illness and accidents, can be a source of profound inspiration and learning.

252. Kopp, Sheldon. *Who Am I . . . Really? An Autobiographical Exploration on Becoming Who You Are*. Los Angeles, CA: Jeremy P. Tarcher, Inc., 1987.
The author writes about the profundity and randomness of life's experiences. The goal of the work is to help explore one's inner self.

253. Kuenning, Delores. *Life after Vietnam: How Veterans and Their Loved Ones Can Heal the Psychological Wounds of War*. New York: Paragon House, 1991.
This book is aimed at veterans who experience Post-traumatic Stress Disorders. The effects of these disorders on relatives are also ex-plored. The book offers advice for resolving guilt and grief for those af-fected by the Viet Nam War experience.

254. LaBerge, Stephen. *Lucid Dreaming: The Power of Being Awake and Aware in Your Dreams*. Los Angeles, CA: Jeremy P. Tarcher, Inc., 1986.
The author feels dream research shows how to wake up one's dreams without disturbing the dream state. Strategies are offered to gain control over and determine the content of one's dreams.

255. Lee, John. *The Flying Boy: Healing the Wounded Man*. New York: New Means Press, 1987.

> This book is a record of one man's search for "true masculinity." The author discusses how he has moved out of codependent and addictive relationships. The work is designed for men and women who have grown up in dysfunctional families, and are now ready for some fresh insights into their past and present pain.

256. Lee, John. *At My Father's Wedding: Reclaiming Our True Masculinity*. New York: Bantam, 1991.

> The author illustrates the benefits of men's groups and the "camp-out and inner journey" gathering that he conducts. The work covers the wounds often inflicted on men by their fathers. Advice is provided for developing "true masculinity."

257. Lerner, Rokelle. *Affirmations for the Inner Child*. Deerfield Beach, FL: Health Communications, Inc., 1989.

> Offered are messages and suggestions aimed at adults who have unfinished childhood issues. The author offers ways in which one can learn skills to reparent–to become a loving parent of our internal children–including the infant and the toddler.

258. Levin, Pamela. *Becoming the Way We Are: An Introduction to Personal Development in Recovery and in Life*. New York: Directed Media, 1985.

> This work deals with the scripts we use to try to cope with our lives and the six stages of the cycle of development. Tools are provided to aid individuals in realizing their own inherent wisdom.

259. Levin, Pamela. *Cycles of Power: A User's Guide to the Seven Seasons of Life*. Deerfield Beach, FL: Health Communications, Inc., 1988.

> This book tries to unveil the process of life as a cyclic pattern through the seven seasons to regain power over one's own life. The work offers the predictable changes in life that appear as threatening crises.

260. McCullough, Christopher J. *Always at Ease*. Los Angeles, CA: Jeremy P. Tarcher, Inc., 1990.

> Over 84 million Americans suffer from social anxiety in some form, whether it is meeting new people, dating, or speaking to the public. Social anxiety can cause one to lose opportunities, including career advancement. The author explains how one can treat the psychological roots of social anxiety; these treatments include the use of case histories, exercises, and quizzes.

261. Miller, Joy. *Addictive Relationships: Reclaiming Your Boundaries.* Deerfield Beach, FL: Health Communications, Inc., 1989.

      The aim of this work is to help one claim one's personal boundaries. The author feels that if we have lost ourselves along the way, it is probably because we have given ourselves away. Approaches are offered for examining where one is, where one wants to go, and how to know when one has arrived. The theme of the work is to move away from addictive love styles in order to find one's true self.

262. Miller, Joy. *My Holding You Back Up Is Holding Me Back: Recovery from Over Responsibility and Shame.* Deerfield Beach, FL: Health Communications, Inc., 1990.

      This work explores the problems related to those who value others over their own selves. The consequences of over responsibility can result in poor physical and emotional health. The author attempts to show how to stop taking care of others and to start taking care of oneself.

263. Nachmanovitch, Stephen. *Free Play: The Power of Improvisation in Life and the Arts.* Los Angeles, CA: Jeremy P. Tarcher, 1991.

      The inner sources of spontaneous creation are explored. Strategies for contacting and strengthening one's own creative powers are explored. The book's purpose is to increase one's understanding, joy, responsibility, and peace.

264. Namka, Lynne. *The Doormat Syndrome.* Deerfield Beach, FL: Health Communications, Inc., 1989.

      The focus of this work is on codependency. The author attempts to encourage one to break the cycle of learned helplessness, to stand up and ask for what one wants. Work sheets, visualization exercises, and meditations are included in the book.

265. Peck, M. Scott. *The Road Less Traveled.* New York: Touchstone Books, 1988.

      Suggestions are offered for confronting and resolving one's problems. This process, according to the author, will enable one to reach a higher level of self-understanding.

266. Pollard, John. *Self-Parenting: The Complete Guide to Your Inner Conversations.* New York: Generic Human Studies, 1987.

      This book is designed to provide direct and practical self-parenting methods. The author contends that by using the dynamics of inner conversation, individuals can discover love, support, and nurture themselves.

267. Rankins, Zoe. *Messages from Anna: Lessons in Living . . . Santa Claus, God, and Love.* Deerfield Beach, FL: Health Communications, Inc., 1992.

Having made peace with God and Santa, the title character begins a quest for the meaning of the word "love." The story takes her search to a small Texas Gold Coast town where she meets a wise elderly woman who shares her lessons for living a loving life.

268. Rico, Gabriele Lusser. *Pain and Possibilities: Writing Your Way through Personal Crisis.* Los Angeles, CA: Jeremy P. Tarcher, Inc., 1991.

Techniques for healing emotional pain are offered. The author suggests that people must name their pain, face it, and own it through the use of expressive language, before they can deal with it effectively.

269. Riley, Mary. *Corporate Healing Solutions to the Impact of the Addictive Personality in the Workplace.* Deerfield Beach, FL: Health Communications, Inc., 1990.

According to this work, national surveys show that between 78 and 85 percent of today's workers find neither joy nor satisfaction in their work places. The author suggests that the individual take responsibility for unproductive habits, and that both employees and employers return to stressing the value of productivity.

270. Robinson, Bryan E. *Soothing Moments: Daily Meditations for Fast-Track Living.* Deerfield Beach, FL: Health Communications, Inc., 1990.

This is a book designed to help one deal with life's problems through meditation. The goal of the work is to help individuals deal more effectively with the fast-paced and high-pressured lifestyles of the modern world.

271. Robinson, Bryan E. *Heal Your Self-Esteem: Recovery from Addictive Thinking.* Deerfield Beach, FL: Health Communications, Inc., 1991.

The author stresses the importance of positive self-esteem. Ten principles for healing are offered that aim at helping one develop new attitudes toward life that improve one's self-esteem.

272. Robinson, Bryan. *Stressed Out? A Guidebook for Taking Care of Yourself.* Deerfield Beach, FL: Health Communications, Inc., 1991.

This work is designed to help one evaluate one's stress quotient. The guidebook provides techniques on how to achieve a balanced, satisfying lifestyle.

273. Rosellini, Gayle, and Mark Worden. *Taming Your Turbulent Past: A Self-Help Guide for Adult Children.* Deerfield Beach, FL: Health Communications, Inc., 1987.

This is a guide for helping individuals deal with anger, and the power of forgiveness, fear, and self-esteem, as well as the problem of always needing to please. Illustrated are approaches to escape pain of growing up in an alcoholic or chemically dependent home.

274. Saltzman, Amy. *Downshifting: Reinventing Success on a Slower Track.* New York: HarperCollins Publishers, Inc., 1992.

   The goal of this work is to show how one can achieve professional happiness on a slower track. The work is designed to help those who wish to make major changes in their lives.

275. Sanford, Linda T., and Jane Donovan. *Women and Self-Esteem.* New York: Viking Penguin, 1985.

   This work examines how women's harmful attitudes about themselves are shaped. Offered are steps to change negative attitudes with the goal of building women's self-esteem.

276. Satir, Virginia. *Self-Esteem.* Berkeley, CA: Celestial Arts, 1975.

   The author focuses on the self-worth of the individual in modern society. The work is designed for those who are looking for new hope, new possibilities, and new positive feelings about themselves.

277. Satir, Virginia. *Making Contact.* Berkeley, CA: Celestial Arts, 1976.

   This work is aimed at helping individuals understand their full potential and improve interaction with others. Basic techniques are offered for making contact with others.

278. Satir, Virginia. *Your Many Faces.* Berkeley, CA: Cestial Arts, 1978.

   This book is designed to help the reader open doors and to make changes in one's life. The goal of the work is to help individuals make contact with the innermost self.

279. Satir, Virginia. *Meditations and Inspirations.* Berkeley, CA: Celestial Arts, 1985.

   Based on the author's workshops, this work provides a series of meditations used by the author to help others enhance the self.

280. Schenkel, Susan. *Giving Away Success.* New York: HarperCollins Publishers, Inc., 1990.

   This is a work that tries to help women change their careers and move toward a more successful life.

281. Silverstein, Lee M. *Consider the Change: The Choice Is Yours.* Deerfield Beach, FL: Health Communications, Inc., 1986.

   Getting stuck with one's own denial and delusion is the focus of this book. Outlined are pathways for personal growth through humility and a searching for honesty. The work is designed to help people make changes in their lives.

282. Simmermacher, Donald. *Self-Image Modification: Building Self-Esteem.* Deerfield Beach, FL: Health Communications, Inc., 1989.

>   This book is designed for those who would like to develop a more positive self-image and self-esteem. Offered are systematic approaches aimed at actualizing human potential and growth.

283. Stark, Amy. *Because I Said So: Childhood Dynamics and Office Politics— How You Can End Negative Influences and Take Charge of Your Career.* New York: Pharos, 1992.

>   The author illustrates how early family influences often interfere with office relationships and career goals. Tools are offered for helping overcome these obstacles.

284. Stuart, Mary S., and Lynnzy Orr. *Otherwise Perfect: People and Their Problems with Weight.* Deerfield Beach, FL: Health Communications, Inc., 1987.

>   This book explores problems ranging from anorexia to obesity, to codependency and its origins in the dysfunctional family. The authors provide a clear explanation of the complex varieties of eating disorders and how to cope with them successfully.

285. Subby, Robert. *Lost in the Shuffle.* Deerfield Beach, FL: Health Communications, Inc., 1987.

>   This is a story about those who seek to find themselves, and break free of their troubled past and their present addiction to rules by which the codependent lives.

286. Taylor, Cathryn L. *The Inner Child Workbook: What to Do with Your Past When It Just Won't Go Away.* Los Angeles, CA: Jeremy P. Tarcher, Inc., 1991.

>   This interactive workbook attempts to teach how to heal one's inner child. A step-by-step guide is offered to reparent the inner child during the first seven stages of life: as an infant, a toddler, a young child, a grade-school child, a young teen, a young adolescent, and a young adult. Writing, drawing, communication, and other activities are the tools presented for helping one heal the inner child.

287. Taylor, Jeremy. *Where People Fly and Water Runs Uphill: Using Dreams to Tap the Wisdom of the Unconscious.* New York: Warner, 1992.

>   The author covers the importance of dreams. This work suggests that dreams help us to understand the meaning of events in our lives. It concludes that dreams are messages from our unconscious that help to make us whole and help heal the self. Techniques are offered for recall and how the group process is useful for understanding dreams.

288. Taylor, Shelley E. *Positive Illusions: Creative Self-Deception and the Healthy Mind.* New York: Basic Books, 1989.

  A psychologist argues that positive self-enhancing illusions about the self can promote mental and physical well-being. The author is attempting to move the field of psychology to revise the way it thinks about mental health.

289. Thompson, Keith (ed.). *To Be a Man: Developing Conscious Masculinity.* Los Angeles, CA: Jeremy P. Tarcher, Inc., 1991.

  The new male is the focus of this work. Such issues as suppressed wildness, grief, shame, and deeper aspects of masculinity are explored, including competition, success, sports, war, fatherhood, and relationships. The book attempts to raise consciousness of males.

290. Twerski, Abraham. *I'd Like to Call for Help, but I Don't Know the Number: The Search for the Spiritual Self.* New York: Pharos Books, 1991.

  This work explores the search for spirituality in everyday life. The author tries to illustrate how the process of spirituality is essential in the 12–step method of recovery from dependency, and how this same process can open the reader to the deeper aspects of life that are often obscured by material concerns.

291. Vaughan, Frances, and Roger Walsh. *A Gift of Healing: Selections from a Course in Miracles.* Los Angeles, CA: Jeremy P. Tarcher, Inc., 1988.

  The author explores the universality of human suffering and the desire for healing. The causes of pain are thought to exist in the human mind rather than in the body. Plans for treatment are offered.

292. Veltman, Jan. *Cry Hope.* Deerfield Beach, FL: Health Communications, Inc., 1988.

  This is a day-by-day guide to help readers gain fuller appreciation of both individual and universal sources of strength, joy, and fulfillment.

293. W., Kathleen, and Jewell E. *With Gentleness, Humor and Love: A 12-Step Guide for Adult Children in Recovery.* Deerfield Beach, FL: Health Communications, Inc., 1988.

  Focusing on adult child issues, such as self-esteem, reparenting the inner child, intimacy, and feelings, this work attempts to teach techniques implementing the 12–step recovery program,

294. Walsh, Anthony. *The Science of Love: Understanding Love and Its Effects on Mind and Body.* Amherst, NY: Prometheus Books, 1991.

  The book offers an examination of the effects of love on one's physical and social well-being. The author covers the emotional, interactional, and physical aspects of love.

295. Ward, Joyce Houser. *Therapy? Unmasking the Fears, Shattering the Myths, Finding the Path to Wellness.* Tarrytown, NY: Wynwood Press, 1992.

        The author argues that self-help can only help so much when one cannot overcome self-destructive behaviors. Oftentimes seeking professional help is difficult because of the stigma attached to seeking such help. Steps are covered that help one decide on therapy, including how one should choose a therapist. The pain that emerges during therapy is also discussed.

296. Wegscheider-Cruse, Sharon. *Choicemaking: For Co-dependents, Adult Children and Spirituality Seekers.* Deerfield Beach, FL: Health Communications, Inc., 1985.

        The author attempts to guide one through personal transformation by improving one's ability to conduct choice making. The work suggests that effective choice making will empower the individuals in their daily lives.

297. Wegscheider-Cruse, Sharon. *Learning to Love Yourself: Finding Your Self-Worth.* Deerfield Beach, FL: Health Communications, Inc., 1987.

        According to this text, self-worth is a choice, not a birthright. Approaches are offered to help one move from low self-esteem to the realization of one's own self-worth. The author concludes that one does not have to follow the family tradition of addiction or compulsion.

298. Wegscheider-Cruse, Sharon. *The Miracle of Recovery: Healing for Addicts, Adult Children and Co-dependents.* Deerfield Beach, FL: Health Communications, Inc., 1989.

        This work is meant to help readers take another look at their history and learn to reframe their thinking about life experiences. Strategies are offered to embrace the positive aspects of experience, and to realize the strength and growth that can come from adversity.

299. Wegscheider-Cruse, Sharon, and Joseph Cruse. *Understanding Co-Dependency.* Deerfield Beach, FL: Health Communications, Inc., 1990.

        This work explores the origins, nature, and effects of codependency. A framework is offered for placing past history and present environment in the proper perspective in order to build a happy, healthy life.

300. Weiss, Laurie. *An Action Plan for Your Inner Child: Parenting Each Other.* Deerfield Beach, FL: Health Communications, Inc., 1991.

        This work attempts to show how crucial it is for adult children to cultivate and nourish their inner child with unconditional love. A plan is offered that sets up a personal parenting program for learning to give and receive appropriate parenting, and learning to develop mature relationships with others.

301. Weiss, Laurie. *I Don't Need Therapy but ... Where Do I Turn for Answers?*
Deerfield Beach, FL: Health Communications, Inc., 1991.
    This book provides answers to questions often asked by recov-
ering adult children and includes problem–solving techniques. The goal
of the author is to help individuals get unstuck and move on with their
lives.

302. Weiss, Laurie, and Jonathan B. Weiss. *Recovery from Co-dependency: It's
Never Too Late to Reclaim Your Childhood.* Deerfield Beach, FL:
Health Communications, Inc., 1989.
    According to the authors, when one has been brought up with
life-repressing decisions, the adult child recognizes something is not
working. The work tries to show how to change decisions, and live differently and fully.

303. Westin, Jeane Eddy. *The Thin Book.* Minneapolis, MN: CompCare
Publishers, 1989.
    The focus of this work is to offer advice on losing weight. The
author offers techniques that helped her lose weight. The work also presents information on self-understanding and self-awareness.

304. Wills-Brandon, Carla. *Where Do I Draw the Line: How to Get Past Other
People's Problems and Start Living Your Own Life.* Deerfield Beach,
FL: Health Communications, Inc., 1991.
    This work is designed for those who are listening to the prob-
lems of others while neglecting themselves. It attempts to offer strategies for developing healthy personal boundaries. Also included is how
one can do self-analysis through looking at one's childhood years.

305. Wilson, Glenn D. *Your Personality and Potential: The Illustrated Guide to
Self-Discovery.* New York: HarperCollins Publishers, Inc., 1992.
    This book examines the ways in which individual personalities
develop, the advantages and problems inherent in the different personality types, the range of emotions experienced by all human beings, and
what to do when emotional problems get out of hand.

306. Woititz, Janet G. *Struggle for Intimacy.* Deerfield Beach, FL: Health
Communications, Inc., 1985.
    This work is designed for those who wish to develop more in-
timate relationships. The book argues that developing intimate relationship is not as tough as many feel, and the author also illustrates how to
get what one wishes from relationships.

8

Serious Illness

The way in which experience is perceived influences the way problems of individuals are defined and treated. As Thomas and Thomas (1928) conclude, in their *definition of the situation*, if a situation is perceived as real, it will be acted on as being real. For example, if a therapist were strongly grounded in Freudian theory, he or she would define a problem such as depression quite differently from the way a behaviorist would define the problem of depression. Both would also use very different methods for intervention. In the area of health, the beliefs and values that shape the practitioner's worldview will greatly influence his or her definition of health and how health-related concerns are treated.

There are three ways that one can look at the problem of health: the *disease model, illness model*, and *sickness model*. The approach used for defining health has a tremendous effect on the assessment and treatment process. For example, if one uses a disease model, health is viewed strictly in terms of the presence or absence of clearly identifiable physical signs and symptoms. If one approaches the issue of health from an illness model, he or she may be grounded in looking at not only physical symptoms but also the psychosocial aspects of health. What constitutes health strongly shapes how it is defined and, if nonhealth is present, how one treats a problem.

A disease model is based on the physical aspect of the person. Disease is a biomedical concept that refers to the physiological features of nonhealth. As would be suspected, a disease model for understanding health has numerous limitations. Unfortunately, this approach continues to be the dominant model for the delivery of health care in the United States (Illich, 1975). The major criticisms of the model are as follows:

1. It is grounded in the "germ theory" for explaining disease, and lacks utility for understanding the multiple causes for assessing and treating chronic illness.

2. The model relies on the effectiveness of differential diagnosis when there is poor reliability among those making diagnoses for physical and mental disease.

3. It seeks a single best treatment to eradicate the cause of chronic illness, whereas most illnesses have multiple causes.

4. This approach results in the dehumanization of health care because of the overreliance on various technologies and overspecializations in the field of health.

5. It promotes authoritarian relationships between practitioners and patients in which the locus of responsibility is removed from the patient.

6. The model acknowledges only the physical aspects of disease, and does not address the psychosocial dimension of assessment and treatment.

7. It is a model of disease care delivery, not health care, and virtually ignores efforts to improve health and prevention of illness.

It becomes clear from the criticisms of the disease model that patients are at a distinct disadvantage because of the authoritarian nature of the approach, and that they are really seen as passive participants in the assessment and treatment process.

An illness approach to understanding health is very different from the disease model. For example, an illness can exist whether a disease is present or absent. If an individual defines him or herself as ill, even though physical symptoms are not present, an illness does exist. This may well be defined as a lack of health. Even though an illness is often assumed to be caused by a disease, there is speculation that if one defines the self as ill, these subjective feelings can foster disease. Rogers, Dubey, and Reich (1979) concluded that subjective feelings of illness may influence changes in the body's immune system, thus promoting the changes for disease to occur.

The sickness model is grounded in the concepts of status, roles, and social identity. This model is based in the field of sociology, and largely views health or the lack of health as being a label created by the larger society. The process of defining someone as sick can happen regardless of whether an illness or disease is present or absent. Minuchin (1974) in his work focuses on the psychosomatic aspect of sickness as defined by the family system. Parson's (1951) work presents a highly developed model of sickness that is grounded in a sociological perspective. The major components of the model are as follows. The sick person:

1. Is not responsible for the condition and cannot get better by an act of self-motivation.

2. Is entitled to some exemptions from normal social activities based on the severity and nature of the illness.

3. Does not like being ill and wants to get better.

4. Must seek competent professional help to get better.

As pointed out by Minuchin (1974), much of one's ability to cope with sickness or illness is affected by one's ability to adapt to his or her social environment. This position is also clearly an important part of Parson's (1951) perspective on health. What this means is that a supportive social environment will result in individuals who have been labeled as sick being better able to adapt and cope with disease and illness. Those environments that are not supportive of sickness will result in poor adaptation for ill individuals.

All of the models for defining health have limitations. However, the disease model does appear to offer little for those concerned with self-help as an important tool in maintaining health, and in treating disease or illness. The component that is clearly lacking in the disease model is the social and subjective nature of health. Both of these critical aspects of health are dealt with far more effectively in the illness and sickness models. Antonovsky (1979) offers helpful insight into how health can be better understood when looking to the psychosocial aspects of sickness and illness.

Antonosky (1979) argues very effectively that health cannot be understood using a pathological orientation, or disease model. He suggests that, instead, one should use a "Dis-ease-Ease" continuum. Antonosky found that nearly one-half of the population will suffer from some form of illness or disease. Some of these conditions will be disabling. Given the nature of illness and disease, and the large numbers of people that are affected, it is very limiting to view sickness or health from a disease perspective, because it places health and disease dichotomously. Health is, instead, according to Antonosky, a highly relative issue that is influenced by genetics as well as one's social environment. Furthermore, health is largely defined by social and cultural factors.

Interesting enough, Antonovsky also suggests that health cannot be solely viewed as a dependent variable. Health as an independent variable may directly affect one's total life experiences, including physical disease. Health, for example, may be the prime reason determining if a person is susceptible to bacterial pathogens that are present in all individuals. In this sense, health and disease form a transaction where each influences the other. Antonovsky (1979) concludes that his "Dis-ease-Ease" continuum allows one to assess health (or disease) in a global fashion that includes the following:

1. Pain level present, from none to severe.

2. The degree of functional limitation, ranging from none to severe.

3. The implications of the prognosis, ranging from minor to life-threatening.

4. What actions must be taken for treatment, ranging from none to immediate.

Through using the above assessment criteria, Antonovsky concludes that 384 possible profiles can be developed to identify one's level of health. This is far from the dichotomous perspective of health versus disease advocated by the disease model.

As suggested earlier, self-help plays an important role in the treatment of illness or sickness if one views these problems from psychosocial and societal perspectives. The self-help books presented in this chapter largely reinforce a more dynamic orientation for dealing with illness, in particular serious illness. It should be noted that none of the works included deny the importance of the biological basis to illness or sickness, but instead recognize the importance of defining health from a biological, psychological, and sociological perspective. Such a view, as suggested by Antonovsky (1979), offers a more holistic view of health that reinforces the active participation of the patient in the assessment and treatment process.

REFERENCES

Antonovsky, A. (1979). *Health, stress, and coping.* San Francisco, CA: Jossey-Bass.

Illich, I. (1975). *Medical nemesis: The expropriation of health.* London: Calder & Boyars.

Minuchin, S. (1974). *Families and family therapy.* Cambridge, MA: Harvard University Press.

Parsons, T. (1951). *The social system.* New York: The Free Press.

Rogers, M. P., D. Dubey and P. Reich (1979). The influence of the psyche and the brain on immunity and disease susceptibility. *Psychosomatic Medicine,* 41, 147–164.

Thomas, W. I., and E. S. Thomas (1928). *The child in America.* New York: Knopf.

BOOKS ON SERIOUS ILLNESS

307. Arno, Peter S., and Karyn Feiden. *Against the Odds: The Story of AIDS Drug Development, Politics, and Profits.* New York: HarperCollins Publishers, Inc., 1982.

> Information on the testing of drugs such AZT, ddl, bactrin, gancyclovir, pentamindine, and compound Q is offered. The role of government, pharmaceutical companies, activists, and patients in the politics related to these drugs is presented.

308. Baur, Susan. *The Dinosaur Man: Tales of Madness and Enchantment from the Back Ward.* New York: HarperCollins Publishers, Inc., 1991.

> This book is based on the real–life experiences of those who have been hospitalized for schizophrenia. Many of the patients in the book are aware of their illness, and others often cannot distinguish be-

tween reality and illusion. The book attempts to provide insight into mental illness.

309. Bernstein, Richard K. *Diabetes: The Glucograf Method for Normalizing Blood Sugar*. Los Angeles, CA: Jeremy P. Tarcher, Inc., 1989.

This is a book designed to help diabetics self-monitor blood glucose levels. Information is provided on diet, nutrition, and exercise.

310. Broida, Helen. *Coping with Stroke: Communication Breakdown of Brain Injured Adults*. Austin, TX: Pro-Ed, 1979.

Information and guidance are offered to victims of stroke. A question-and-answer format is utilized. The author responds to questions dealing with speech difficulties, writing, gestures, time, and changes that brain damage brings to families.

311. Budnick, Herbert N. *Heart to Heart: A Guide to the Psychological Aspects of Heart Disease*. New York: Health Press, 1991.

Heart disease can be an emotionally crippling disease. This work shows how one can work effectively with individuals experiencing heart disease. The author illustrates the importance of the family in the treatment process. The work offers advice to heart disease victims and their families.

312. Callen, Michael. *Surviving AIDS*. New York: HarperCollins Publishers, Inc., 1991.

A chronicle of the struggle of long-term AIDS survivors is covered. The book attempts to offer a message of help and inspiration for everyone affected by AIDS.

313. Carroll, David. *Living with Parkinson's*. New York: HarperCollins Publishers, Inc., 1992.

This is a guide for patients and caregivers based on the methods developed at a national center on aging.

314. Craig, Jean. *Between Hello and Goodbye: A Life-Affirming Story of Courage in the Face of Tragedy*. Los Angeles, CA: Jeremy P. Tarcher, Inc., 1991.

A wife (the author) and her husband react to his terminal cancer. The author offers a firsthand tour of the labyrinth that is the modern medical establishment and attempts to explore the myths that surround it.

315. Dachman, Ken, and John Lyons. *You Can Relieve Pain: How to Use Guided Imagery to Reduce Pain or Eliminate It Completely!* New York: HarperCollins Publishers, Inc., 1991.

This work focuses on the problem of chronic pain. It offers methods using thoughts or mental scenes associated with a desired mental state, and literal imagery that centers on the organ, muscle, or other body part that is experiencing pain.

316. Dilley, James W. *Face to Face: A Guide to AIDS Counseling.* Berkeley, CA: Celestial Arts Publishing, 1989.
    This is a guide to the emotional problems of AIDS, designed for both the patient and the professional and developed by the AIDS Health Project at the University of California, San Francisco. It covers such topics as the emotional responses to HIV seropositivity, neurological problems in AIDS, and the special needs of the variety of affected populations.

317. Dreher, Henry. *Your Defense against Cancer: The Complete Guide to Cancer Prevention.* New York: HarperCollins Publishers, Inc., 1990.
    This is a book designed for people who want to be healthy. The work is designed for the layperson.

318. Fiore, Neil A. *The Road Back to Health: Coping with the Emotional Aspects of Cancer.* Berkeley, CA: Celestial Arts Publishing, 1990.
    The author presents his story of how he dealt with cancer. Topics covered include how to face the fear of diagnosis and reduce stress of therapy; how to select a doctor; and how to evaluate treatments and cope with side effects.

319. Garrison, Judith G., and Scott Sheperd. *Cancer and Hope: Charting a Survival Course.* Minneapolis, MN: CompCare Publishers, 1989.
    Written for those with cancer and their families and friends, this work is about taking control of one's life and participating in one's own healing. The author provides the metaphor of a sea journey to help the cancer patient. The work includes exercises, work sheets, visualizations, and thoughts to get well by.

320. Garrison, Judith Garrett, and Scott Sheperd. *I Will Live Today!* Minneapolis, MN: CompCare Publishers, 1990.
    Affirmations are offered on building a strong spirit and healthy attitude, to help individuals cope with chronic and life-threatening illness. There is a focus on the creation of positive emotional energy to enhance the quality of life and strengthen opportunities for recovery. It attempts to encourage readers to visualize peace and restoration.

321. Goldstein, Jay, and Robert Wolenik. *Could Your Doctor Be Wrong?* New York: Pharos Books, 1990.
    The author focuses on the problem of misdiagnosed symptoms and treatment of the wrong illnesses. A series of case histories is offered that helps the reader understand the problems related to misdiagnoses.

322. Gross, Amy, and Dee Ito. *From Diagnosis to Recovery: Women Talk about Breast Surgery*. New York: HarperCollins Publishers, Inc., 1991.

      This is a guide to the problems associated with breast surgery. The reactions to and feelings about breast surgery are presented.

323. Gross, Amy, and Dee Ito. *Women Talk about Gynecological Surgery: From Diagnosis to Recovery*. New York: HarperCollins Publishers, Inc., 1992.

      This guide for women describes procedures of all types of gynecological surgery and retells the experiences of women who have been through them in their own words. A detailed glossary of terms and a section on patient's rights are presented.

324. Hargove, Ann C. *Getting Better: Conversations with Myself and Other Friends While Healing from Breast Cancer*. Minneapolis, MN: CompCare Publishers, 1985.

      Designed for women facing breast cancer, this book attempts to offer practical ways to help mend body and spirit.

325. Hoffa, Heynn, and Gary Morgan. *Yes You Can: A Helpbook for the Physically Disabled*. New York: Pharos Books, 1990.

      For the more than 40 million physically disabled in the United States, this book offers advice for the handicapped on all aspects of day-to-day living, including obtaining a degree and a job, traveling, improving one's social life, looking after personal health and appearance, and finding where to go for help.

326. James, John S. *Aids Treatment News, Volume 1, Issues 1 through 75*. Berkeley, CA: Celestial Arts Publishing, 1991.

      This work offers standard and experimental therapies for AIDS and its associated illnesses. The text is designed for the layperson.

327. James, John S. *AIDS Treatment News, Volume 1, Issues 76 through 125*. Berkeley, CA: Celestial Arts Publishing, 1991.

      Complementing the author's earlier work, this one presents more recent findings on AIDS treatment and research.

328. Jampolsky, Gerald G. *Another Look at the Rainbows*. Berkeley, CA: Celestial Arts Publishing, 1983.

      This work is written by and for children who have siblings afflicted with life-threatening illness. The drawings in the book are done by children, and demonstrate the pain, hurt, and fears they feel resulting from the knowledge that their siblings are seriously ill.

329. Jovanovic, Lois, June Biermann, and Barbara Toohey. *The Diabetic Woman: All Your Questions Answered*. Los Angeles, CA: Jeremy P. Tarcher, Inc., 1988.

     Diabetes complicates the problems posed by marriage, career, motherhood, pregnancy, and menopause. Practical answers are offered for women diabetics.

330. Kaplan, Andrew S., and Gray William, Jr. *The TMJ Book*. New York: Pharos Books, 1988.

     This is a book that overviews the mysterious disease that affects over 10 million Americans. It provides explanation of how to recognize symptoms and seek treatment of disorders of the jaw. It includes an explanation of costs for treatment and insurance options, and offers a program of self-help.

331. Kerman, D. Ariel, and Richard Trubo. *The H.A.R.T. Program: A Comprehensive Guide to Normalizing Your Blood Pressure and Becoming Medication-Free*. New York: HarperCollins Publishers, Inc., 1992.

     This is a guide that offers methods for relaxation and stress management assisted by temperature feedback. The goal of the book is to help hypertensives take control of their own health.

332. Klein, Allen. *The Healing Power of Humor*. Los Angeles, CA: Jeremy P. Tarcher, Inc., 1988.

     This book is designed to help one turn negatives into positives. The author attempts to provide practical advice as to the fundamental importance of laughter and humor.

333. Krementz, Jill. *How It Feels to Live with a Physical Disability*. New York: S & S Trade, 1992.

     This is a series of life stories of children ranging from ages 6 to 16 years. They share how it feels to live with a disability. The work is aimed at parents and professionals who work with children with disabilities.

334. Krippner, Stanley, and Alberto Villoldo. *The Realms of Healing*. Berkeley: CA: Celestial Arts Publishing, 1986.

     This is a study that explores what occurs during healing. The authors analyze the secrets of the shaman and medicine man from a scientific and psychological standpoint to discover just what underlies the healing effected.

335. Long, James W. *The Essential Guide to Prescription Drugs 1991: Everything You Need to Know for Safe Drug Use.* New York: HarperCollins Publishers, Inc., 1992.

This is a comprehensive reference on widely used prescription drugs available to consumers.

336. Mikluscak-Cooper, Cindy, and Emmett E. Miller. *Living in Hope.* Berkeley, CA: Celestial Arts Publishing, 1991.

This is a 12–step program for people with AIDS, ARC, or HIV infection. This work offers the 12-step approach to help cope with the AIDS epidemic. Daily affirmations and guided imagery are offered in the text.

337. Nelson, John E. *Healing the Split: A New Understanding of the Crisis and Treatment of the Mentally Ill.* Los Angeles, CA: Jeremy P. Tarcher, Inc., 1991.

Serious mental illness is the focus of this book. Drawing upon brain science, psychiatry, transpersonal psychology, and patient case histories, the author offers new strategies for dealing with serious mental illness.

338. Oyle, Irving. *The New American Medicine Show.* Berkeley, CA: Celestial Arts Publishing, 1981.

This is an investigation into the dimensions of twenty-first century medicine. The study explores the potential of using the mind in the healing process. The author suggests that treating disease and illness through the mind is a concept and practice that continues to grow in appeal within the field of medicine.

339. Pantano, James A. *Living with Angina.* New York: HarperCollins Publishers, Inc., 1991.

A cardiologist outlines the causes, effects, and treatment of angina. The author offers approaches for helping patient and doctor work together to deal with the problem of angina.

340. Podell, Richard. *Doctor, Why Am I So Tired?* New York: Pharos Books, 1988.

This is a guide to the medical causes of chronic fatigue. The author explains the major causes of tiredness, including medication, improper nutrition, sleep disorders, and stress. Solutions to these problems are offered.

341. Reed, Paul. *Serenity* (2nd ed.). Berkeley, CA: Celestial Arts Publishing, 1990.

> This work discusses the emotional turmoil of facing HIV disease and AIDS. The work is designed to provide counseling for early intervention, including coping with learning of one's HIV seropositivity and struggling with the will to live.

342. Reed, Paul. *The Q Journal.* Berkeley, CA: Celestial Arts Publishing, 1991.

> This is the journal of a writer who, while mourning the death of his lover, embarked on an experimental HIV treatment program with the Chinese drug, Compound Q.

343. Royak-Schaler, Renee, and Beryl Lieff Benderly. *Challenging the Breast Cancer Legacy.* New York: HarperCollins Publishers, Inc., 1992.

> Insight is presented into the problem of breast cancer. This work is based on a pioneering study from the Georgetown University Comprehensive Breast Center.

344. Ryan, Regina Sara. *The Fine Art of Recuperation: A Guide to Surviving and Thriving: Illness, Accidents, or Surgery.* Los Angeles, CA: Jeremy P. Tarcher, Inc., 1985.

> This is a guide aimed at providing a happier and more productive recovery. The author attempts to show how one can turn time in recovery from a difficult, upsetting, and boring event into a positive experience.

345. Salzer, Linda P. *Surviving Infertility: A Compassionate Guide through the Emotional Crisis of Infertility.* New York: HarperCollins Publishers, Inc., 1991.

> This is a work that examines the social and emotional problems of infertility. This book attempts to provide sympathetic and direct advice to the reader.

346. Schoenewolf, Gerald. *Jennifer and Her Selves.* New York: Donald I. Fine, 1991.

> This book covers the author's work with a client who has attempted suicide. The client suffers from a multiple personality disorder. The author illustrates the various problems encountered when working with the multiple personality disorder.

347. Seeland, Irene, and Samuel Klagsbrun (eds.). *The Final 48 Hours: Observations on the Last Days of Life.* New York: Charles Press Publishers, 1991.

> These essays are intended to help individuals in grieving. Observations about death and dying are offered by professionals, including physicians, psychologists, and hospice workers. The book is intended to help professionals work with those who have lost a loved one.

348. Serinus, Jason. *Psycho-Immunity and the Healing Process* (3rd ed.). Berkeley, CA: Celestial Arts Publishing, 1990.

Numerous individuals with HIV disease seek alternative therapies whether as an adjunct to conventional medical care or as an independent path toward healing. This work offers a different way of understanding AIDS and immune dysfunction, and includes thorough discussion of alternative treatments.

349. Shtasel, Philip. *Medical Tests and Diagnostic Procedures: A Patient's Guide to Just What the Doctor Ordered.* New York: HarperCollins Publishers, Inc., 1991.

This is written for the layperson as a guide to understanding what to expect when a doctor orders one to have a diagnostic test or make a visit to a specialist. The goal of the book is to help patients be better–informed consumers.

350. Siegel, Bernie S. *Love, Medicine and Miracles: Lessons Learned about Self-Healing from a Surgeon's Experience with Exceptional Patients.* New York: HarperCollins Publishers, Inc., 1988.

This book covers the process of self-healing and cases of remission of serious illness. Strategies are offered for patients coping with serious illness.

351. Siegel, Bernie S. *Peace, Love and Healing: The Bodymind and the Path to Self-Healing: An Exploration.* New York: HarperCollins Publishers, Inc., 1990.

This work stresses the importance of learning how to talk to our inner selves, and give ourselves healing messages through meditation, visualization, and relaxation. The author explores the unity between the mind and body, and the way to self-healing with inspiring stories of patients and their remissions from serious illness.

352. Simonton, O. Carl, Stephanie Matthews-Simonton, and James Creighton. *Getting Well Again: A Step-by-Step Self-Help Guide to Overcoming Cancer for Patients and Their Families.* Los Angeles, CA: Jeremy P. Tarcher, Inc., 1989.

This book examines how patients can deal with cancer. Psychological techniques are offered.

353. Williams, Wendy. *The Power Within: True Stories of Exceptional Patients Who Fought Back with Hope.* New York: HarperCollins Publishers, Inc., 1990.

Readers are introduced to patients who refused to accept their prognosis. Case studies are offered that cover the lives of people who fought back with hope against serious illness.

9

Social Relationships

Chess and Norlin (1991, p. 159) define the term *social relationship* as "the cognitive and affective connection existing between two or more people in which each takes the other(s) into account in their thoughts and in relevant aspects of behavior." Presently, there is tremendous emphasis on improving the critical aspects of social relationships, in particular, the cognitive and affective aspects, as well as improving sensitivity to others.

Social relationships are critical because they give life and depth to the human experience. They offer great potential for enormous gain in one's personal growth and enjoyment in life. However, if they are hindered, the quality of life and the human experience suffer. Most people work very hard at improving their social relationships with others; however, within our culture, there is very little available to teach one how to nurture relationships so we can realize their full potential.

The critical components that one must focus on to improve social relationships are self-awareness, awareness of others, and communication. In this chapter, a number of self-help books are offered that are aimed at improving each of these aspects. The following will stress how each of these components is critical to the quality of a social relationship.

Self-awareness is essential to helping one relate to others. How one views the self is often how he or she will view others. Even though complete awareness of the self is never possible, it is clear that improving awareness of one's self will improve awareness of others and their feelings (Miller, Nunnally, and Wackman, 1975).

It is often difficult to develop self-awareness because certain past events are too painful to deal with. Remaining unaware in order to avoid painful feelings of the past usually does not work well for developing quality relationships. At times, these feelings may be unconscious; thus, one may not even be aware of their existence. Miller, Nunnally, and Wackman (1975, pp. 87–88) suggest that limited self-awareness can stem from the following:

1. At times for certain individuals, thinking and doing are confused. That is, rather than owning one's awareness and using all of it to make responsive decisions, an individual's thoughts are censored and unacceptable ones are pushed out of awareness, but not necessarily out of the person's life. Thus, the thoughts continue to influence feelings, intentions, and actions.

2. Into each relationship that one enters, one carries a host of preconceived notions based on past experiences. Over time one develops so many preconceptions and value judgments that it is impossible to be aware of all of them. Even though one is not aware of these preconceived notions, they still exert influence over one's awareness. Some of these preconceptions are useful, and others are not. In order to improve social relationships, it is important to stop and to get in touch with these preconceived notions.

3. Often one is aware of certain aspects of the self but will maintain them as "hidden interpretations." Consequently, for example, we do not let our partner know what we really think about the self, about him or her, or about the relationship that binds each to the other. If this process extends over time, thoughts are held out of fear, protection, mistrust, or dishonesty. This form of limited self-awareness is particularly damaging to relationships because potentially useful information is consciously withheld. In essence, the growth process within a relationship is stifled by choice.

It becomes clear that limited awareness of self not only thwarts individual growth and development, but also prevents individuals from growing in relationships with significant others. In essence, if one can improve awareness of the self, the overall quality of one's life will also be enhanced.

Self-awareness and awareness of others are processes that complement each other. As suggested, quality relationships are difficult to create if one does not have insight into the self as well as sensitivity to others. What awareness of others involves is appropriate perception of another's sensations, thoughts, feelings, intentions, and actions. If these perceptions are accurate, the ground work for developing a quality relationship is possible.

Miller, Nunnally, and Wackman (1975, pp. 124–126) offer a number of techniques for helping one develop awareness of others. Many of these are techniques used by clinicians to explore the inner world of clients. These include:

1. When sending a message to another, many people report that hearing their message reflected back helps them to see if they left out any important information. Using such a technique helps to ensure that each person is understanding the other in an appropriate fashion.

2. Serving as a "sounding board" for others helps one to develop insight into another and also helps another work through a problem. In a certain sense, one is acting as a resource person, helping him or her sort out or get in touch with his or her feelings, ideas, and intentions.

3. When one wants to send a positive intimate message to another, one must think about the impact it would have on the self. If one has limited self-awareness, it is difficult to hear and accept this kind of message, and obviously hard to send such a message.

4. Awareness of others also means that one has a notion of when to deal with an issue. If one lacks sensitivity to another, that is, he or she is not in touch with another's feelings and sense of self, issues may be brought up at the wrong time and place. Such an occurrence may result in destructive interaction that limits the growth and development of a relationship.

5. Sharing meaning about sensations, thoughts, feelings, intentions, and actions can put one in touch with not only another but also the self. Through the process of shared meaning, one can learn what the other senses, thinks, feels, and intends to do. Ultimately, this information will help to ensure that individuals are in touch with not only the self but also others.

The communication process is clearly critical to developing awareness about others and the self. Quality social relationships are dependent on understanding how the communication process works.

Good communication, both verbal and nonverbal, is critical to enhancing relationships. Individuals who have problems in building relationships with others often do not realize that much of the communication process is nonverbal. Thus, one may send a very complimentary verbal message; however, the nonverbal message sent may be incongruent with the verbal message. This kind of double binding results in the receiver of a message not knowing what the sender is attempting to communicate. Consequently, if one wishes to build quality relationships, one must not only work at understanding the importance of nonverbal messages, but also attempt to ensure that one's verbal and nonverbal communications are congruent.

Satir's (1976, p. 92) work offers a number of suggestions that can help one to ensure that communication flows clearly between the self and another. These include the following:

1. One must manifest the self clearly to another. What this means is that verbal and nonverbal messages are congruent.

2. It is critical to be in touch with one's inner self, thus allowing one's self to know openly what he or she thinks and feels.

3. Being able to see and hear what is outside the self as differentiated from the self is critical to sending clear messages to another.

4. One should attempt to behave toward another person as someone who is separate and unique.

5. Treat the presence of differentness as an opportunity to learn and explore rather than as a threat or signal of conflict.

What Satir is clearly suggesting is that communication between the self and others is critical to social relationships. Okun and Rappaport (1989. p. 93) summarize Satir's ideas as follows. First, within the social relationship, each person should be able to report congruently, completely, and obviously on what he or she sees and hears, feels and thinks about himself or herself and others. Second, each person within the social relationship should be related to in terms of his or her uniqueness, so that decisions are based on explorations and negotiation rather than in terms of power. Last, differences within the social relationship should be openly acknowledged and used for growth and development.

This chapter offers a number of self-help books that focus on improving social relationships. Many of these titles highlight the importance of self-awareness, awareness of others, and the communication process as critical areas for understanding and improving social relationships. The following books can be useful resources for helping one to improve relationships with others. Therapists will find many of these titles to be useful supports to the treatment process when working with clients who are attempting to improve relationships with partners, spouses, and significant others.

REFERENCES

Chess, W., and J. Norlin. (1991). (2nd ed.). *Human behavior and the social environment: A social systems model.* Needham Heights, MA: Allyn and Bacon.

Miller, S., E. Nunnally, and D. Wackman. (1975). *Alive and aware: Improving communication in relationships.* Minneapolis, MN: Interpersonal Communications Programs, Inc.

Okun, B., and I. Rappaport. (1989). *Working with families: An introduction to family therapy.* North Scituate, MA: Duxbury Press.

Satir, V. (1967). (rev. ed.). *Conjoint family therapy.* Palo Alto, CA: Science and Behavior Books.

BOOKS ON SOCIAL RELATIONSHIPS

354. Beck, Aaron T. *Love Is Never Enough: How Couples Can Overcome Misunderstandings and Solve Problems through Cognitive Therapy.* New York: HarperCollins Publishers, Inc., 1989.
    This work examines how lack of communication, misunder-

standing, and other common problems in marriage can be overcome through actual conversations from the author's clinical practice. The author builds his work on cognitive therapy.

355. Bengis, Ingrid. *Combat in the Erogenous Zone: Writings on Love, Hate and Sex*. New York: HarperCollins Publishers, Inc., 1991.

This book is about relationships between men and women. The major focus of the work is on the problems related to these relationships.

356. Eyler, David R., and Andrea P. Baridon. *More Than Friends, Less Than Lovers: Managing Sexual Attraction in the Workplace*. Los Angeles, CA: Jeremy P. Tarcher, Inc., 1991.

The problems associated with sexual attraction in the work place are covered. As women and men increasingly find themselves working and traveling side by side as cocreators, sales teams, bosses, and secretaries, sexual attraction is likely to increase. This book offers strategies for dealing with problems related to sexual attraction in the work place.

357. Fast, Julius. *Making Body Language Work in the Workplace*. New York: Viking, 1991.

The author details how body language works and its relevance to one's culture. The work attempts to provide ways in which one can create a successful personal image. The aim of the author, in particular, is to help people succeed in the work place.

358. Haynes, Jody, and Maureen Redl. *Smart Love: A Codependence Recovery Program on Relationship Addiction Support Groups*. Los Angeles, CA: Jeremy P. Tarcher, Inc., 1989.

This is a workbook designed to help one recover from relationship addiction. The book is intended to provide readers with heightened awareness of negative behavior, a greater ability to replace old habits with new positive ones, and guidelines for developing positive relationships.

359. Hite, Shere, and Kate Colleran. *Good Guys, Bad Guys: The Hite Guide to Smart Choices*. New York: Carroll and Graf Publishers, 1991.

This book provides approaches to helping male-female relationships work. Advice is given on when to abandon a relationship, male-female compatibility, and the importance of communication. Information on relationships involving friendship is offered.

360. Hornstein, Harvey A. *Knight in Shining Armor: The Man behind the Myth: Frog Princess, Sleeping Beauties, and Other Destructive Types.* New York: Morrow, 1991.

    The author concludes that men must be knights in shining armor in their relationships with women. The work places men in such categories as educators who must guide women. Interviews with men are offered that illustrate the so-called Man-Servant Syndrome. The author concludes that relationships between men and women based on the Man–Servant Syndrome will not work.

361. Johnson, Barbara L. *Brothers and Sisters: Getting Back Together with Your Adult Siblings.* New York: Prometheus Books, 1991.

    Time and circumstances often separate adult siblings from the closeness they may have once felt. The author attempts to illustrate how one might rebuild these lost relationships through a series of strategies based on the author's case studies.

362. Kritsberg, Wayne. *Healing Together: A Guide to Intimacy and Recovery for Co-Dependent Couples.* Deerfield, CA: Health Communications, Inc., 1989.

    This is a book that attempts to offer practical advice. The author explains to the reader why he or she gets into dysfunctional and painful relationships, and then gives advice on how to move the relationship toward health.

363. Leonard, George B. *Adventures in Monogamy: Exploring the Creative Possibilities of Love and Sexuality.* Los Angeles, CA: Jeremy P. Tarcher, Inc., 1992.

    This book redefines the meaning of love, sex, and romance in the modern era. The author argues for a renewal of a deeper, more meaningful kind of erotic love akin to the most moving creative and spiritual experience.

364. Lerner, Harriet Goldhor. *The Dance of Anger.* New York: HarperCollins Publishers, Inc., 1989.

    The author attempts to illustrate how women can use anger productively to clarify and change relationships rather than remain stuck in patterns of ineffective fighting, blaming, or emotional distancing. The work is designed for both men and women.

365. Lerner, Harriet Goldhor. *The Dance of Intimacy.* New York: HarperCollins Publishers, Inc., 1990.

    This work provides an outline of the steps to take so that good relationships can be strengthened and difficult ones can be healed. Combining advice with case studies, the author offers strategies for enhancing intimate relationships.

366. Levine, Judith. *My Enemy, My Love! Men-Hating and Ambivalence in Women's Lives.* New York: Delacorte, 1992.

This book offers a postfeminist treatise that attempts to illustrate the reasons for gender stereotypes and why man hating exists in our culture. The book presents the problems of men as defined by women. Women and their conflicts are explored. A final section of the book offers ways men and women can live in greater harmony.

367. Mandel, Bob. *Two Hearts Are Better Than One.* Berkeley, CA: Celestial Arts Publishing, 1986.

This is a handbook on creating and maintaining a lasting and loving relationship. Included are affirmations and personal growth exercises to facilitate this goal.

368. Napier, Augustus Y. *The Fragile Bond: In Search of an Equal, Intimate and Enduring Marriage.* New York: HarperCollins Publishers, Inc., 1990.

Designed for both professionals and laypersons, the work attempts to improve the marriage of individuals. The author uses case studies and his own life experiences as a guide to achieve this effort.

369. Norwood, Robin. *Women Who Love Too Much: When You Keep Wishing and Hoping He'll Change.* Los Angeles, CA: Jeremy P. Tarcher, Inc., 1985.

This is a book about relationships. The author offers help and hope for women obsessed with relationships that are doomed to failure.

370. Ray, Sondra. *Loving Relationships.* Berkeley, CA: Celestial Arts Publishing, 1990.

This work attempts to illustrate how to find, achieve, and maintain a deeper, more fulfilling relationship with one's mate. The work encourages self-awareness through using affirmations and emotional exercises to improve relationships with significant others.

371. Rhodes, Sonya. *Second Honeymoon: A Pioneering Guide for Reviving the Midlife Marriage.* New York: Morrow, 1992.

Many marriages during midlife reach a point of instability; consequently, divorce becomes a distinct possibility. The author suggests that many problems associated with marriages during the midlife point are predictable. These include psychological changes, loss of parenting role, sexual problems, and severe illness. The author concludes that these predictable crises can be a catalyst for changing and rebuilding a marriage. Advice is offered for improving marriage during the midlife period.

372. Ricketson, Susan C. *Dilemma of Love Healing: Co-dependent Relationships at Different Stages of Life.* Deerfield Beach, FL: Health Communications, Inc., 1989.

   Practical suggestions are offered in this book that help individuals distinguish between healthy love and codependent behavior. The author attempts to help individuals learn to love their original family in a new and healthy way, and fill their lives with satisfying intimate relationships.

373. Tannen, Deborah. *You Just Don't Understand: Women and Men in Conversation.* New York: Ballantine, 1991.

   The author combines research with anecdotes to illustrate important conversational style differences between men and women. Based on the premise that the risk of ignoring differences is greater than the danger of naming them, the work attempts to offer insight into improving professional and personal relationships.

374. Taylor, Richard. *Having Love Affairs.* Amherst, NY: Prometheus Books, 1990.

   The author argues that many love affairs, whether extramarital or outside established relationships, are stable relationships. The work provides insight into those relationships that are often viewed as unacceptable and suggests that they may provide fulfillment to those involved.

375. Tessina, Tina. *Gay Relationships: How to Find Them, Improve Them, How to Make Them Last.* Los Angeles, CA: Jeremy P. Tarcher, Inc., 1989.

   This is a step-by-step guide to help in making relationships work for gay men and women. The book suggests that like all relationships, gay relationships can and do survive most problems, as long as partners are willing to work at them.

376. Wegscheider-Cruse, Sharon. *Coupleship: How to Build a Relationship.* Deerfield Beach, FL: Health Communications, Inc., 1988.

   This book analyzes relationships that individuals often experience in their lives. Advice on how to build a healthy, intimate relationship is presented.

377. Welwood, John. *Journey of the Heart: Intimate Relationships and the Path of Love.* New York: HarperCollins Publishers, Inc., 1991.

   The author attempts to reveal how learning to use whatever difficulties we face in relationships can provide opportunities for enrichment and growth. The work concludes that through improving relationships one will experience personal and spiritual discovery.

378. Williamson, Marianne. *A Return to Love: Reflections on the Principles of a Course of Miracles*. New York: HarperCollins Publishers, Inc., 1992.

This work explores how people can improve their lives and their relationships with others. The author suggests that returning to the heart and recognizing love as a potent force are the critical factors for obtaining inner peace and change.

379. Wills-Brandon, Carla. *Is It Love or Is It Sex?* Deerfield Beach, FL: Health Communications, Inc., 1989.

Many people experienced difficulty at some time in their primary relationships. Some can work through the problems, and others find themselves confused, lonely, and frustrated. The author examines relationships in depth. Utilizing self-analysis and self-discovery, the author attempts to guide the reader through relationship problems toward the solutions.

380. Wills-Brandon, Carla. *Learning to Say No: Establishing Healthy Boundaries*. Deerfield Beach, FL: Health Communications, Inc., 1990.

This work focuses on the concept of *boundaries*, a term that has emerged out of systems theory. The author presents examples and self-evaluation exercises that will encourage the reader to identify, realize, evaluate, and then accept healthy boundaries, and continue to growth socially and psychologically.

381. Woititz, Janet G., and Alan Garner. *Lifeskills for Adult Children*. Deerfield Beach, FL: Health Communications, Inc., 1990.

This book is designed to help individuals stand up for themselves without losing their tempers and to make decisions without second-guessing. The author teaches these and other interpersonal skills that can make one's life easier while improving one's sense of self-worth. Examples are provided to help clarify the lessons, and exercises are given for practicing new skills.

10

Divorce and Blended Families

The family is the most important social institution in society. As has been well documented (Pardeck, 1981), the family is under tremendous pressure. Furthermore, the family has lost many of its traditional functions (Pardeck, 1990); however, it continues to be the core social institution for meeting the socialization and psychological needs of family members.

Recent research suggests the family needs additional support (Pardeck, 1990), and this is particularly the case in the United States. Unlike most advanced industrial nations, the United States lacks a consistent, coherent family policy. Numerous families in the United States lack adequate health care, social services, such as day care, and income supports. Many of the problems associated with family life in the United States could be reduced if the United States had a family policy.

Given the lack of support for the family system within the United States, the breakdown of the family appears to be quite logical. The divorce rate within the United States is the highest in the developed world (Pardeck, 1990). It has been effectively argued that if the United States had a developed family policy, the divorce rate would decrease. Furthermore, other factors associated with family breakdown, including child abuse and neglected family violence, would also be reduced. Consequently, those who work with families have to use creative and innovative approaches to help families deal with the crisis of divorce in a society that offers little support. Most people who divorce in the United States remarry, and many of these blended families include children from prior marriages. Bibliotherapy can be a useful tool for helping families deal with divorce and remarriage.

Goode (1976, p. 555) provides critical facts about divorce that help to understand the various aspects of this phenomenon. These are as follows:

1. *Age of Spouses*. Divorce most commonly occurs when the partners are in their 20s.

2. *Length of Engagement.* The longer a couple's engagement, the less likely it is that they will divorce.

3. *Length of Marriage.* Most divorces occur within the first two years of marriage. There is also an increase in divorce after children leave the home.

4. *Social Class.* Divorce is more likely to occur in the lower socioeconomic classes.

5. *Education.* Divorce is higher among those with fewer years of education. However, divorce is more likely to occur when the wife's education level is higher than the husband's.

6. *Residence.* Divorce rates are higher in urban areas and lower in rural areas.

7. *Second Marriages.* The more often individuals divorce, the more likely it is that they will divorce again.

8. *Religion.* The more religious an individual is, the less likely it is that he or she will divorce. Divorce rates are generally higher among Protestants than among Catholics or Jews. The divorce rates increase with interfaith marriages.

A key concern for parents who divorce is the impact that it will have on children. Wallerstein and Kelly (1980) found that divorce does indeed have a number of negative consequences for children. In particular, children often have problems acknowledging the divorce, resolving loss related to divorce, resolving anger and self-blame, accepting the permanence of the divorce, and finally, forming relationships with others. More recent research by Wallerstein and Blakeslee (1989) suggests that many of these feelings are long–term. For example, they found that children of divorce who had grown to adulthood had not resolved the anger related to the family breakdown. Many of the adult children were underachievers and continued to have problems forming relationships. These findings suggest that divorce is not an easy process, and that many issues need to be resolved for not only children but also parents.

Thompson and Rudolph (1992, pp. 386–389) suggest that parents and practitioners working with children of divorce may benefit from the following suggestions:

1. Talk with the child about the divorce. Explain to children that the divorce is not their fault. Ensure that the child's fears related to the divorce are dealt with, and avoid blaming or criticizing one parent over the other.

2. Plan ways that will make the child's life stable even though many changes are taking place. Household routines, school schedules, and

consistent discipline will help children understand that the world has not fallen apart. Teachers and other significant adults should be involved in the divorce as support systems.

3. Do not use children as a go-between for parents or to find out what the other parent is doing. One must remember that children of divorce love both parents and are torn between conflicting loyalties.

4. Arrange for visits from the absent parent to ensure that children know they are loved by both parents. The absent parents should always attempt to make visits with their children if they have committed to these visits.

5. Talk with the children about what is likely to happen in the future. Involve them in the planning without overwhelming them with the problems related to the divorce. Children, like adults, need to know what to expect.

6. Children experiencing divorce are still children at a particular stage of development. Do not ask children to assume responsibility beyond their capabilities of development. Examples might be asking them to babysit younger children when they are not capable of doing so or making them take on excessive household chores.

Finally, parents and practitioners must realize that the child's adjustment after divorce will take time and require efforts by all significant adults in the child's life. Thompson and Rudolph (1992) found that group counseling was helpful not only to children of divorce but also to their parents. Clinicians can use books as a useful adjunct to the group intervention process.

As the family system changes within the United States, one must remember that the intact nuclear family has been viewed as the *ideal* family form. As the divorce rate increases as well as the number of parents who remarry each year, this traditional view of the family should be considered. According to Thompson and Rudoph (1992), approximately one–third of children born in the 1980s will live in blended families. The blended family is a system in which one adult has had a child prior to the couple's marriage (Kupisch, 1984).

Early research by Stinnet and Walters (1977) reported the following concerning the blended family:

1. The integration of the blended family is easier if the initial family breakdown is due to divorce versus death.

2. Children and their parents come to blended families with unrealistic expectations that love and happiness will rapidly occur.

3. Children in blended families often feel stepparents favor their own children over them.

4. Most children continue to love and admire the absent parent.

5. Male children appear to adjust better to the blended family than female children.

6. The younger the child, the more likely it is that a child will accept the stepparent.

These early findings suggest that the creation of the blended family involves major changes in the lives of children and their parents. Also, the creation of the blended family is a process that involves stress and strain for all family members involved, including the extended family.

The joining of two families into one creates problems for both children and their parents. For example, children coming to the blended family often must cope with the effects of the biological parents' divorce. For parents, the stigma of failure in their first marriage may also be a problem. Given these conditions, members of blended families bring a unique set of problems to the therapeutic setting. Practitioners who work with blended families must work with adults and children who are often still dealing with problems related to family breakdown. Furthermore, they must work with problems with the creation of a blended family that has a structure, interactional modes, and functioning very different from families of first marriages.

Kupisch (1984) concludes that the blended family is not viewed as equal to first-marriage families. Often religious groups view the blended family differently from first-marriage families. Stepparents frequently do not have the same legal rights as parents from first marriages. Socially, stepparents are often viewed as extra baggage at school, family, and other social functions. It is also not unusual for school activities to be built around first marriages, such as Father's Day, Mother's Day, or related school functions that honor parents. The lack of acceptance of blended families by the larger society only adds to the problems that they must confront on an ongoing basis.

Gardner's (1984) research focuses on the disturbances that children in blended families must confront. He found that anger and hostility are very common among children in blended families. This anger is directed toward not only parents in their blended family but also the absent biological parent. In other words, children in blended families must continue to deal with their parents' divorce, as well as the feelings of anger often associated with being part of a blended family. Furthermore, in first-marriage families, sibling rivalry is almost always present; it is greatly intensified in the blended family because of the fact that unrelated children are brought together who are supposed to behave like biological siblings, an obviously unrealistic expectation. Love and respect in blended families take a great deal of time, and realistically may never occur between stepsiblings. Finally, Fuller (1988) argues that research focuses entirely too much on the negatives associated with the blended families. She suggests that blended families provide many strengths for children. For example, flexibility is promoted because children must learn to adjust to new situations; they are also provided with multiple role models, and with additional siblings for learning and enjoyment.

Kupisch (1984) presents a number of approaches clinicians can use to help blended families improve their social functioning:

1. Help stepparents understand that their role is largely negotiated by both adults and children. They must be realistic about their role as stepparent, and realize that it takes time and effort for their new role to be clarified and understood by stepchildren.

2. Even though their first marriage has ended, stepparents must realize that they continue to have financial responsibilities to their children. Also, stepparents must realize that social relationships that existed prior to the blended family still remain.

3. Parents in blended families must find ways to ensure that contact with absent parents continues. Arguments and custody battles over visitation rights are very common, and children often become pawns in the conflict between parents.

4. Open communication is critical in the blended family. Parents must realize that the number of authority figures and loyalties increases in the blended family, and that children must be able to express their feelings about the conflict that may result from this situation. Discipline of children is especially difficult because the noncustodial parent may discipline differently than the stepparent.

5. Practitioners must help stepparents and their children realize that love is not automatic in the blended family, and that it will only evolve out of patience and love.

6. Clinicians must help stepparents and their children realize that time and work are needed to develop emotional bonds for all blended family members. Parents are entitled to a quality relationship with their new spouse, and children must feel a sense of security in the blended family.

Clinicians who work with blended families must realize that there are many myths concerning these families. Awareness of the strengths and weaknesses of the blended family must be understood. Like all families, blended families have unique needs that must be met to ensure that family members experience growth, development, and love.

The self-help books in this chapter are designed to help parents and children deal with the unique problems associated with family breakdown and the creation of the blended family. The following titles can be used in individual counseling, group settings, or simply as a resource for families to understand better problems associated with divorce and remarriage.

REFERENCES

Fuller, M. (1988). Facts and fictions about stepfamilies. *Education Digest*, 54(2), 52–54.

Gardner, R. (1984). Counseling children in stepfamilies. *Elementary School Guidance and Counseling*, 19, 40–49.

Goode, W. (1976). Family disorganization. In *Contemporary social problems*, 4th ed., ed. Robert K. Merton and Robert Nisbet, 511–555. New York: Harcourt, Brace, Jovanovich,

Kupisch, S. (1984). Stepping into counseling with stepfamilies. *The Virginia Counselor's Journal*, 12, 38–43.

Pardeck, J. T. (1981). Some barriers to a national policy for the American family. *International Journal of Family Therapy*, 8, 56–61.

Pardeck, J. T. (1990). An analysis of the deep structure preventing the development of a national policy for children and families in the United States. *Early Child Development and Care*, 57, 23–31.

Stinnet, N., and J. Walters. (1977). *Relationships in marriage and family*. New York: Macmillan.

Thompson, C., and L. Rudolph. (1992). *Counseling children*. 3rd ed. Pacific Grove, CA: Brooks Cole Publishing Company.

Wallerstein, J., and S. Blakeslee. (1989). *Second chances*. New York: Ticknor & Fields.

Wallerstein, J., and J. Kelly. (1980). *Surviving the breakup: How children and parents cope with divorce*. New York: Basic Books.

BOOKS ON DIVORCE AND BLENDED FAMILIES

382. Arendell, Terry. *Mothers And Divorce: Legal, Economic, and Social Dilemmas*. Berkeley: University of California Press, 1986.

> This work explores the numerous issues related to divorce, including legal and economic. The author bases the book on an empirical study of the problem of divorce.

383. Belli, Melvin M., and Mel Drantzler. *Divorcing*. New York: St. Martin's Press, 1990.

> This book is written by a family therapist and an attorney. Offered are the legal and emotional problems associated with divorce.

384. Berman, Claire. *Adult Children of Divorce Speak Out*. Minneapolis, MN: CompCare Publishers, 1992.

> Insights are offered for children who are experiencing divorce. The work presents interviews with men and women of all ages that have experienced divorce, including insights into developing new relationships.

385. Berstein, Anne C. *Yours, Mine and Ours: How Families Change When Remarried Parents Have a Child Together*. New York: Macmillan Publishers, 1989.

This book is written by a family therapist. The work is based on a study of the dynamics of blended families.

386. Brown, Laurence Krasny, and Marc Brown. *Dinosaurs Divorce: A Guide for Changing Families*. Boston, MA: Atlantic Monthly Press, 1986.

This text attempts to get to the heart of the feelings and problems common to children during and after divorce. The authors try to offer practical advice to children.

387. Burns, Cherie. *Stepmotherhood: How to Survive without Feeling Frustrated, Left Out, or Wicked*. New York: Harper and Row Publishers, 1985.

This is a book to help women improve their parenting in stepfamilies. Many of the myths surrounding stepmothers are covered.

388. Burt, Mala Schuster, and Roger B. Burt. *What's Special about Our Stepfamily*. New York: Dolphin Books, 1983.

This book stresses that divorce is never easy, nor is the establishment of a blended family. The authors present the unique problems of children in blended families. Included are fill-in-the-blank questions for children to answer about blended families and other related activities.

389. Christansen, C. B. *My Mother's House, My Father's House*. New York: Atheneum, 1989.

A child from a divorced family tells her story about how she spends four days at her mother's house and three days at her father's. Both houses are homes, but neither parent will visit the other.

390. Clapp, Genevieve. *Divorce and New Beginnings: An Authoritative Guide to Recovery and Growth, Solo Parenting, and Stepfamilies*. New York: Wiley, 1992.

This is a self-help book on divorce. The effects of divorce are covered, including the legal, emotional, and economic. Various kinds of parenting are explored—part-time, single, and stepparenting.

391. Diamond, Leonard. *How to Handle Your Child Custody Case: A Guide for Parents, Psychologists, and Attorneys*. Amherst, New York: Prometheus Books, 1989.

This guide is for individuals who wish to gain insight into the custody process. It provides samples of custody contracts and details the workings of the court system.

392. Diamond, Susan Arnsberg. *Helping Children of Divorce: A Handbook for Parents and Teachers.* New York: Schocken Press, 1985.
    This book is for parents and teachers who are attempting to work with children experiencing divorce. The focus of the work is on helping children deal with common psychological and social problems related to divorce.

393. Dinkmeyer, Don, Gary McKay, and Joyce L. McKay. *New Beginnings: Skills for Single Parents and Stepfamily Parents.* Champaign, IL: Research Press, 1987.
    This manual presents new skills and ideas that focus on the needs of today's single and stepfamily parents. Case examples and illustrations are presented. Contents include self-esteem, relationship and behavior, personality, and emotional development.

394. Drescher, Joan. *My Mother's Getting Married.* New York: Dial Press, 1986.
    This book presents a picture-book format that describes a common problem in today's society–remarriage of parents. The child in the book resents the parent's remarriage.

395. Einstein, Elizabeth. *The Stepfamily: Living, Loving, and Learning.* New York: Macmillan Publishing, 1982.
    The author stresses that each stepfamily must integrate its past loss into the carving of its own future despite the complex relationships and often ambivalent emotions. The author explores this core issue through chapters that include information on family roles, resolving old relationships, myths and attitudes about blended families, and stepchildren as scapegoats.

396. Felker, Evelyn H. *Raising Other People's Kids.* Grand Rapids, MI: William B. Eermans Publishing, 1981.
    This work covers the struggle of raising nonbiological children. The author attempts to guide stepparents through a series of practical activities that help them improve their role as stepparent.

397. Francke, Linda Bird. *Growing Up Divorced.* New York: Check Fawcett Publishers, 1984.
    This book is based on interviews with children of divorced parents, and offers insights into the social and psychological effects of divorced.

398. Hales, Dianne. *The Family.* New York: Chelshea House Publishers, 1988.
    This work includes chapters on the changing family. Information is provided on the blended family.

399. Keshet, Jamie K. *Love and Power in the Stepfamily: A Practical Guide.* New York: McGraw-Hill, 1987.

> This book includes information on all aspects of creating blended families. Chapters include discussions on parenting after divorce, introducing children to new partners, affection and unification, remarried couples, and the new baby.

400. Kline, Kris, and Stephen Pew. *For the Sake of the Children: How to Share Your Children with Your Ex-Spouse–In Spite of Your Anger.* Rocklin, CA: Prima Publishing, 1991.

> This book is written for those who have experienced divorce. Suggestions are offered for dealing with the pain of divorce and the anger often felt. Strategies are covered for dealing effectively with one's ex-spouse.

401. Krantzler, Mel. *Learning to Love Again.* New York: Harper and Row Publishers, 1987.

> This book analyzes the development of new relationships when old ones have failed. Particular emphasis is on new living arrangements, creating new commitments, and stepchildren.

402. Krementz, Jill. *How It Feels When Parents Divorce.* New York: Knopf, 1984.

> Nineteen boys and girls share the experiences and feelings they had while adjusting to divorced families. The children represent several ethnic groups and a wide range of experiences, ranging from a background of violence in the home to resolution of friendly joint custody.

403. Lindsay, Jeanne Warren. *Do I Have a Daddy? A Story about A Single-Parent Child.* Minneapolis, MN: CompCare Publishers, 1991.

> The work includes resources, drawings, and text to help children adapt to living in single-parent families.

404. Pitzele, Sefra Kobrin. *Surviving Divorce: Daily Affirmations.* Deerfield Beach, FL: Health Communications, Inc., 1991.

> The author attempts to help individuals survive divorce through this text. Advice is offered through affirmations that are designed to ease the pain and restore confidence for those who have experienced divorce.

405. Pogue, Carolyn. *The Weekend Parent: Learning to Live without Full-Time Kids.* Minneapolis, MN: CompCare Publishers, 1992.

> This work attempts to address sensitive issues related to loss or surrender of child custody. These are the personal stories of 20 men and women who have lost custody and subsequently discovered new roles noncustodial parents can play in the lives of their children.

406. Rosin, Mark Bruce. *Stepfatherings' Advice on Creating a New Stepfamily.* New York: Simon and Schuster, 1987.
         This is a book to help men improve their parenting in the blended family. Practical advice is offered to accomplish this process.

407. Sandvig, Karen J. *Adult Children of Divorce: Haunting Problems and Healthy Solutions.* Waco, TX: Word, Inc., 1990.
         Based on exhaustive research and real-life examples (loneliness, low self-esteem, and others), this book shows how to break the cycle and keep these feelings from contributing to dysfunctional relationships a generation later.

408. Schuchman, Joan. *Two Places to Sleep.* Minneapolis, MN: CompCare Publishers, 1979.
         This book is designed to reassure and support children affected by divorce. Information is offered that explains divorce to children and shows how children can still love each parent after divorce.

409. Visher, Emily, and John Visher. *How to Win as a Stepfamily.* New York: Drmbner Books, 1982.
         The emphasis of this work is on the process of creating blended families. Included are chapters on forming new relationships, dealing with former spouses, legal issues, and helping children adjust to the blended family.

410. Wallerstein, Judith, and Sandra Blakeslee. *Second Chances: Men, Women and Children a Decade after Divorce.* New York: Ticknor and Fields, 1989.
         This book presents the economic and psychological effects of divorce on children. The work is based on a study of 60 middle–class divorced families.

411. Wolter, Dwight Lee. *My Child, My Teacher, My Friend: One Man's View of Parenting in Recovery.* Minneapolis, MN: CompCare Publishers, 1991.
         This work is intended for all parents, particularly single parents in recovery and those who grew up in dysfunctional families. Practical help and wisdom concerning family dysfunction are presented.

Author Index

Includes authors and joint authors
Numbers refer to individual entries

Title Index

Numbers refer to individual entries

Subject Index

Numbers refer to individual entries

About the Author

JOHN T. PARDECK is currently on the faculty at Southwest Missouri State University in the Department of Social Work. He is the author of *Child Welfare Training and Practice* (Greenwood, 1982), *Young People with Problems: A Guide to Bibliotherapy* (Greenwood, 1984), *Books for Early Childhood: A Development Perspective* (Greenwood, 1986), *Microcomputers in Early Childhood Education* (1988), and *Child Abuse and Neglect: Theory, Research, and Practice* (1989).